A CENTURY OF EMANCIPATION

THOMAS FOWELL BUXTON

A CENTURY OF EMANCIPATION

JOHN HARRIS

'This country when it stands before history, will stand, when all else has passed away, not by her fleets and her armies and her commerce, but by the heroic self-denying exertions which she has made to put down this iniquitous [slave] traffic.'

LORD ROSEBERY

KENNIKAT PRESS
Port Washington, N. Y./London

A CENTURY OF EMANCIPATION

First published in 1933
Reissued in 1971 by Kennikat Press
Library of Congress Catalog Card No: 72-122864
ISBN 0-8046-1369-9

Manufactured by Taylor Publishing Company Dallas, Texas

KENNIKAT NEGRO CULTURE AND HISTORY SERIES

DEDICATED TO A LADY

As a century of effort to abolish slavery in all its forms drew to a close, the forces engaged against overwhelming odds in the defence of Native Races found their ranks inspirited by a new personality in their midst—a woman with her soul aflame for the succour and freedom of the oppressed had come forward and had thrown herself into the struggle.

Like Florence Nightingale, Elizabeth Fry and Harriet Beecher-Stowe, she lays bold hands upon men and women in every walk of life. She will lay under tribute rulers of the earth as readily as she enlists the help of the widow with her generous mite. Neither physical limitations nor social engagements are permitted to curb her humane activities. She is often the despair of her doctors when at the risk of her own health she undertakes some enterprise in order to save the bodies and souls of others. Such a woman is Lady Simon, and to her this book is gratefully dedicated.

AUTHOR'S PREFACE

THIS book is an attempt to meet what I am told the public demands—'a popular book' setting forth the story of struggles during a hundred years for emancipating child races, backward races, native races from systems either of slavery or of oppression under which they the weaker races have been in the past and are still to-day exploited for selfish ends.

I don't know exactly what constitutes a 'popular book,' but I am told that its first essential is brevity—a book in a chapter, a chapter in a page, a paragraph in a sentence! This task of compression has been no light one. Let the reader imagine what it means to bring within the compass of less than seventy thousand words the suffering, and for the majority untimely death, of at least 25,000,000 human beings during the last hundred years. Millions of them during their short existence had their flesh torn with the lash or their bodies broken under torture; millions again have known no family life; their persons and their labour have been at the disposal of the highest bidder. Any one of the systems of slavery under which they have suffered would require at least one book to itself—and there have been a dozen of them during the hundred years under review.

This book is not merely an attempt to portray

suffering, it is also an attempt to give a brief account of the systems under which these things have been done, and still more an effort to recount the light and shade of the great struggles carried on by a mere handful of earnest souls beginning with Clarkson, Wilberforce, Buxton, Pitt, Sturge, Macaulay, Lushington, Grey, Livingstone, then on to Vandervelde, Dilke, Fox Bourne, Morel, Hodgkin and others.

The book will fail in its purpose if it does not focus public attention on systems of oppression which are in operation *to-day*—Slave systems which hold in bondage over 5,000,000 men, women, boys and girls, every one of whom is a saleable *property*; Labour systems which hold men and women by force or fraud; Land systems which take from the native his only means of economic freedom.

The book shows how those who have struggled and are still struggling with these sordid but powerful forces have never numbered more than a few hundreds. Whilst it may be true that those few hundreds have been men and women of wisdom and influence, yet it is even more true that they have been men and women possessed of souls burning with a spiritual passion for freedom and justice—that was and is their chief source of strength.

If this had not been so, how could they have slain so many Goliaths of greed and cruelty in every decade of the last hundred years, for they have never been equipped with the ample resources of other philanthropic bodies? The splendid missionary work of Great Britain attracts no less than £2,500,000 a year for Protestant missions to preach the gospel of divine forgiveness and love. The great work for the prevention of cruelty to animals, with its generous income of £100,000 a year, is another parallel. But for the purpose of preaching the divine gospel of simple justice for native races and for the prevention of cruelty to the child races of the world, less than £2,000 a year is contributed! Surely a sorry fact which is not less amazing than the splendid victories which have been won, the millions saved from the lash, the chain, the shackle and the gun; the millions whose labour systems have been cleansed from fraud and force, and the millions whose economic freedom has been preserved to them.

In the difficult task of compressing the accumulated mass of material and presenting it within the compass of these 270 pages, I am deeply indebted to my friend and colleague Lady Stewart, who has given her time and talents regardless of many other claims upon her time and energy. But above all, we have shared a personal interest which at a time of exceptional stress and difficulty has been an invaluable comradeship.

To many members of the Buxton and Wilberforce families, particularly to the Earl and Countess Buxton, Lord Noel Buxton, Mr. Travers Buxton and Sir Herbert Wilberforce, we have been much indebted for suggestions, facts and documents, some of which have hitherto been either unpublished or unknown.

JOHN HARRIS.

1933.

CONTENTS

CHAPTER I

ABOLITIONISTS AND EMANCIPATORS

CHAPTER II

ABOLITIONISTS AND EMANCIPATORS

CHAPTER III

ABOLITIONISTS AND EMANCIPATORS

CHAPTER VII

THE AFTERMATH OF SLAVERY—BUXTON'S LAST YEARS

CHAPTER VIII

VICTORIAN STRUGGLES

CHAPTER IX

VICTORIAN STRUGGLES

CHAPTER X

THE SERVITUDE OF RUBBER AND COCOA—THE CONGO

CHAPTER XIV

NATIONAL TO INTERNATIONAL EFFORT

CHAPTER XV

SLAVERY TO-DAY

A CENTURY OF EMANCIPATION

CHAPTER I

Abolitionists and Emancipators

'They conquer who believe they can.'

Wilberforce and his Colleagues — Spiritual Forces — 'Property' alarmed — The Asiento — Attitudes of: Burke, Pitt, Fox, Duke of Wellington, Joseph Sturge, John Gladstone—The Religious Bodies.

One hundred years ago the nobler elements in Britain were at last beginning to prevail against a monstrous evil—Slavery. For two hundred years the unholy practice of trading in our fellows had been extending its tentacles through every avenue of life, corrupting British men and women, choking the arteries of the social and even of the religious life of the nation. The story of the years of struggle during 1787 to 1833 under the leadership of Wilberforce, Buxton and their friends 'may probably,' as Lecky says, 'be regarded as among the three or four perfectly virtuous acts recorded in the history of nations."

It was not merely that these efforts brought to an end so gigantic a system of oppression and terminated barbarities of so atrocious a nature, but the movement had positive effects in British national life. As

Professor Rex Coupland says, in his admirable life of Wilberforce, it

> founded in the conscience of the British people a tradition of humanity and of responsibility towards the weak and backward black peoples whose fate lay in their hands. And that tradition has never died. . . . It was nothing less, indeed, than a moral revolution; and those who see the world's life as a whole, as an intricate, shifting complex not only of states and nations but of continents and races, discordant, yet interdependent, heterogeneous, yet all belonging to one human family, will give a high place in history to the Englishman who did so much to bring about that revolution.

This struggle in due course gave birth to a movement in Great Britain which for more than a hundred years has dominated British Colonial policy; produced administrators like Cromer, Lugard, Macaulay, Hubert Murray, George Grey and General Gordon; given to religious missions stout-hearted champions for upright dealing with native races such as Livingstone, Smith, Knibb, Shrewsbury, Moffatt and Austin, and at home given rise to a race of men and women whose sacred fire has always leapt into flaming activity whenever any system has developed which has shown the slightest tendency to reviving a commerce in human beings.

The spiritual and mental atmosphere of the period was almost overwhelmingly unfavourable to these stout-hearted Abolitionists. When the apparently insuperable obstacles which stood in their way are considered—the spiritual atrophy of the Churches, the callousness to human suffering in general, the public indifference to slavery, and the immensely powerful vested interests which supported slavery—it becomes a moot question whether in 2,000 years the spirit of

Christianity which at all times governed the actions of the Abolitionists has ever accomplished anything greater. Although it was Christianity which ultimately won the victory, it was only after a crusade lasting nearly fifty years. That victory lies to the eternal credit of Clarkson, Sharp, Wilberforce, Buxton, Sturge, Lushington and their colleagues.

How tremendous the odds against the Abolitionists, how deep-seated the evil in our national life, may be gathered from the fact that even the Abolitionists themselves did not at first grasp a truth set forth by Buxton and emphasised many years later at the Jubilee of the Anti-Slavery Society by King Edward VII, then Prince of Wales, that the only sure way to abolish slave-trading was to abolish slave-owning.

They first strove for Abolition of the Slave Trade, which Wilberforce, at the age of forty-eight, carried through in 1807. The campaign for the Emancipation of the Slaves did not really begin until about 1820. The Slave Trade had in the meantime actually increased, and the checking of its international development was one of the aims of the Duke of Wellington.

Against the Emancipators [1] were arrayed first the 'West Indians,' the representatives of the strongest vested interest of that day, known as 'The Trade.' They prophesied that Abolition would spell the ruin of London, Liverpool and other cities. The Abolitionists were vigorously opposed by cities in their corporate capacity, who were able to draw upon city revenues

[1] Those who sought to abolish the Trade were known as Abolitionists; those who sought to abolish Slave-owning as Emancipators. In course of time both sections became known as Abolitionists.

for the purpose. It is estimated that the Liverpool Corporation spent more than £10,000 in combating Abolition. The Council presented scores of petitions, employed counsel and paid witnesses and 'delegates' to advance their cause. They conferred the Freedom of the Borough upon those who assisted in combating Abolition. Amongst those so honoured were Hawkesbury (afterwards Lord Liverpool) for his support of the Slave Trade; a piece of plate, value £100, was given to Mr. Penny, one of the 'delegates,' with the Freedom of the Borough to his son. They gave to Mr. Green, another of their 'delegates,' £500; they conferred the Freedom of the Borough upon one eminent person: the box containing his grant of Freedom cost £226, and the illuminated address cost twenty-five guineas! Pamphleteers vilified and slandered the Abolitionists and thundered against the

> Pestilent doctrines of those hot-brained fanatics who, under the vile pretence of philanthropy and zeal for the interests of suffering humanity, preach up rebellion and murder to the contented and orderly negroes in our territories.

Slave-owners attacked Wilberforce for 'having unnaturally gone about stirring up a fermentation.' Wilberforce's personal character and position placed him above the reach of the lower forms of calumny, but the obscure Kentish clergyman, the Rev. W. Ramsay, who, after having spent some years witnessing the cruelties of West Indian slavery, had done more than almost any other man to open the eyes of Wilberforce to its horrors, was safe game, and him they slandered into his grave and publicly rejoiced at having done so. Slavery in their view was 'countenanced by the law of God'—it was better, they asserted, for the negroes to be enslaved under Christian influences in the West Indies than free in heathen Africa; they argued that slavery was not cruel and in any case the West Indies would be ruined if slavery were abolished.

At times they showed an amusing lack of humour, as when 'an old M.P.' gave as an instance of the great benevolence with which the negroes were treated that 'Dr. Dalzell has often taken the irons off his slaves.' On another occasion a gentleman from Mauritius assured Buxton that the blacks there were in fact the happiest people in the whole world, and appealed to his wife: 'Now, my dear, you saw Mr. T.'s slaves. Do tell Mr. Buxton how happy they looked.' 'Well, yes,' innocently replied the lady, 'they were very happy, I'm sure, only I used to think it so odd to see the black cooks chained to the fire-place.'

Property felt itself threatened. The Trade argued that if their property rights in the slaves were abolished and the planting community ruined, all property rights would be endangered. As Earl Buxton has well said:

> Opposition came not only from those personally and pecuniarily interested in the question, but also from those who looked upon the agitation as a 'radical,' rapacious or sentimental attack on a long-established industry, and directed against the sanctity of property, the individual rights of owners, and other vested interests—and in those days, as we realise from the penal code, property was more of a fetish even than it is now. Slavery as an institution was actually defended on religious grounds.[1]

And so, for many years, first the Slave Trade, and when that was abolished, Slavery itself, had the support of a great number of the landowners, country

[1] Introduction to the *Memoirs of Sir T. F. Buxton*, by Earl Buxton, published in Everyman's Library.

squires, and worthy merchants so powerfully represented in Parliament.

The West Indian proprietors included many of the most aristocratic and respectable families in the land, but in profiting by the Slave Trade they were only following earlier and still more exalted forerunners, for when Admiral Sir John Hawkins shipped negroes from Sierra Leone to San Domingo, he had the countenance of Queen Elizabeth. She expressed, indeed, a pious wish that the negroes should not be taken away to labour against their will, but she lent him, for his second venture, her own ship, the *Jesus* of Lübeck, and when he returned to England he had the honour of being received by her and of dining with the Spanish Ambassador.

That worthy and domesticated sovereign, Queen Anne, 'who sometimes counsel took and sometimes tay,' was a party to the infamous Asiento, by which 'Her Britannic Majesty did offer and undertake'—such are the words of the treaty—

> by persons whom she shall appoint, to bring into the West Indies of America belonging to his Catholic Majesty, in the space of thirty years, 144,000 negroes, at the rate of 4,800 in each of the said thirty years; paying, on 4,000 of them, a duty of thirty-three and a third dollars a head. . . . As great profits were anticipated from the trade, Philip V of Spain took one quarter of the common stock, agreeing to pay for it by a stock-note; Queen Anne reserved to herself another quarter (which she subsequently divided between Lady Masham and some of her favourites); and the remaining moiety was to be divided among her subjects. The sovereigns of England and Spain became the largest slave merchants ever known in the history of the world.[1]

[1] Stephens, *The Slave in History*.

But the Royal Family of Great Britain had then, and happily always has had, members who used their great influence for both Abolition and Emancipation. Of these the most constant was the Duke of Gloucester, one of the sons of George III, at whose house Abolitionist meetings were frequently held, who became the first President of the African Society and who spoke courageously for Abolition in the House of Lords.

The West Indian Legislatures disregarded almost all the recommendations for better treatment of the slaves despatched by the Colonial Office, and their powerful representation in Parliament made even sympathetic Colonial Secretaries, like Sir George Murray, in 1825, afraid of 'trouble with the Colonies.'

In Parliament the fight for the Abolition of the Slave Trade lasted 18 years, that for the Emancipation of the Slaves another 26 years. Its delay for so many years was due to the inertia, reaction and lack of imagination of the many little men who refused for a variety of reasons to follow the lead of the few really great men on both sides of the House.

Burke always stood for the Abolition of the Slave Trade, and had contemplated undertaking the task of Abolition himself before he became engrossed in Indian questions. He paid a magnificent tribute to Wilberforce's great speech in 1789, and devoted all his eloquence and powers of reasoning to showing that no threatened loss of commerce could justify the terrible inhumanity of the Trade. 'If some loss there must be, were they not prepared,' he asked, 'to pay the price of virtue?'

William Pitt, the close friend of Wilberforce, made some of the greatest speeches in our Parliamentary history for Abolition, and when, in 1788, Wilberforce was so ill that the doctors despaired of his recovery, he appealed to Pitt to move his proposed Resolution in his place, and Pitt responded nobly.

Fox, on the other side of the House, was equally faithful to the cause, and when, after Pitt's death, he came into power, he at once moved a Resolution in the Commons. He died before Abolition was carried, and during his long illness wished that 'he could go down to the House once more to say something on the Slave Trade.'

Canning, in brilliant and witty speeches, supported the Abolition of the Slave Trade from the beginning, and later favoured Emancipation, although his speech from the Government benches in 1823 showed that he felt how great were the practical difficulties.

To the Duke of Wellington 'the suppression of the Trade was a simple matter of clean humanity,'[1] and although he condemned the Emancipation Bill of 1833 as violating the rights of property, he fought stoutly though unavailingly at the Conference of Paris and Verona for the right to search slave ships and set the slaves free.

So the fight went on. A few noble and great men against the indifference or opposition of the multitude. Year after year the motion for Abolition was defeated, but victory crowned the efforts of Wilberforce when in March, 1807, Abolition was achieved and the stage was set in preparation for Buxton's struggle for Emancipation.

The Abolitionists, whilst supported whole-heartedly by large sections of the Christian Church, could not

[1] R. Coupland, *Wilberforce*.

command its undivided co-operation. The coldness and deadness of eighteenth-century religion still prevailed. Lord Sankey has recently emphasised this. Speaking on the Oxford Movement,[1] 'England,' he said, 'and the whole of the Continent were in a state of unrest, there was moral and national bankruptcy. On Easter Day of 1800 there were only six Communicants at the Annual Communion Service at St. Paul's Cathedral, the parish churches were in a state of neglect, and the services casual and perfunctory.'

As Christianity revived, abhorrence of slavery grew; but it would be equally true to say that the practical Christianity which Wilberforce and Buxton preached and lived, and their call to all Christians to end a system which was the negation of Christian principles, acted as a powerful stimulus to the religious revival.

In America Abolitionists were formally denied Church membership, as Joseph Sturge discovered when he went there in 1841. In England it would be fair to say that the Churches had not awakened to the criminal nature of slavery, and that clergy and ministers had not grasped the fact that the practice of slavery broke every law of the decalogue. Leading families in the Christian Churches were so closely connected with the Slave Trade that it is probable that the average church-goer's attitude was pretty accurately reflected in a letter written by Mr. John Gladstone, father of the future Prime Minister, quoted by Viscount Morpeth in the House of Commons in 1831. John Gladstone, one of the most respected Liverpool merchants, was asked, 'Is slavery, then, to be interminable in our colonies?' And he replied, 'I humbly

[1] *The Times*, November 5, 1932.

conceive that it is not for me to attempt to say when a system should terminate which Almighty God in the Divine Wisdom of His overruling Providence has seen fit to permit in certain climates since the origin and formation of society in this world.'

In the Church of England, as in other bodies, there were a few Abolitionists, but they were at first mere voices crying in the wilderness. As long ago as 1766 Bishop Warburton had proclaimed from the pulpit that 'the infamous traffic for slaves directly infringes both Divine and human law.' Bishop Hanley in 1799, and Bishop Burgess preached the same doctrine, and Bishop Porteous gave Wilberforce steady and consistent support and said that 'perpetual slavery is worse than death.'

Another of the Abolitionists brought anathemas on his head for drawing public attention to the fact that the Society for the Propagation of the Gospel drew part of its revenue from the slave-cultivated Codrington Estates in the West Indies. Others preached and protested, the Rev. Andrew Thomson, D.D., and the Rev. S. C. Wilks amongst them.

But the Quakers and Methodists had led the way long before. To the Quakers belongs the everlasting honour of having been the first Christian community in England, as in America, to make a stand collectively and consistently against this negation of Christianity. As early as 1724 they passed a resolution condemning the Slave Trade and Slavery altogether. In 1758 they warned, and in 1761 disowned, all Friends who continued to participate in the Trade. The Wesleyans, meantime, had followed the lead of the Quakers. In 1739 Whitefield, who was then in America, had plainly hinted, though he had not declared outright, that the Slave Trade was anti-Christian, and in 1774 John Wesley himself entered the lists with his widely read 'Thoughts upon Slavery.' His support of the cause was unfaltering, and a week before his death in 1791 he wrote to Wilberforce, then preparing to move an Abolition Motion in the House of Commons: 'Unless God has raised you up for this very thing, you will be worn out by the opposition of men and devils; but if God be for you, who can be against you? . . . Go on, in the name of God and in the power of His might.'

But although for many years organised Christianity as a whole was predominantly either apathetic or hostile, when at last it was roused it was overwhelming.

Some of the poets and writers came to the aid of the Abolitionists. In America there was Whittier, the friend of Sturge. In Europe there were Pope, Defoe, Thomson, Wordsworth (with his magnificent sonnet to Toussaint l'Ouverture). William Cowper attacked the Slave Trade in 'The Task,' and later wrote three poems, of which the best known is 'The Negro's Complaint.'

The Abolitionists occupied too early a page in history to admit women to any prominent share in their task, for convention still kept them outside public questions. It seems surprising that until the year 1905 the Committee of the British Anti-Slavery Society did not even admit women members. Wilberforce apparently regarded public agitation by women as undesirable, although, as will be seen from a letter written to Buxton in 1820, he placed a high value upon their silent co-operation through prayer. 'In this way the ladies may help us more decorously and consistently than by petitionings or similar obtrusive exhibitions of patriotism. Don't forget this hint. I have a high sense of value of the prayers of real Christians.'

It was Lady Middleton who, when her heart was wrung by what she had heard of the horrors of slavery from the Rev. W. Ramsay, Vicar of Preston, brought him and Wilberforce together at her house at Barham Court, and adding her prayers to Ramsay's eloquence, helped to persuade Wilberforce to make the cause his life work.

Fowell Buxton's mother was a Quaker, and the Quaker women had long been warring, with unshakable quietude, but equally unshakable determination, against slavery. Buxton records that he used to laugh at his sister for refusing to eat sugar (slave-grown, as all sugar was then). 'But,' he added, 'her doing so made me think.' His beloved sister-in-law, Priscilla Gurney, was devoted to the cause of the slaves. She sent for him just before she passed away in 1821, and her last articulate words to him were, 'The poor, dear slaves.' He adds, 'I could not but understand her meaning, for during her illness she had repeatedly urged me to make their cause and condition the first object of my life, feeling nothing so much on her heart as their sufferings.' In 1833, when Buxton presented a petition to Parliament 'from the females of Britain,' 187,000 signatures had been obtained in ten days, and 'the Ladies' Committee had worked from ten in the morning till past nine at night.' Later, Harriet Martineau not only wrote vigorously, but visited North America to help on the cause there.

Thus under the leadership first of Wilberforce and

then of Buxton, a phalanx of noble souls was welded together for the single purpose of combating the crime of trading in human beings. This minority, drawn mainly from the Parliamentary and the religious life of Great Britain, was destined to change the history of nations. They attacked first the Slave Trade; then, with the growth of public opinion, they led the movement triumphantly onward to an attack upon slave-owning in British Dominions. They reaped indeed a more abundant harvest than they had dared to anticipate, for, as the pages of this book show, they laid the foundations of a movement which for a hundred years has been alert to attack any semblance of a return to slavery in British Dominions, and within recent times has generated a powerful international movement against every form of slave-owning, slave-raiding and slave-trading throughout the world.

CHAPTER II

Abolitionists and Emancipators

'They conquer who believe they can.'

Wilberforce and Buxton—Buxton's Family and Early Life—Buxton enters Parliament—Joins Wilberforce—Historic Conference at Cromer Hall—Clarkson on Work of Wilberforce and Buxton.

WILBERFORCE the Abolitionist and Buxton the Emancipator were men of an extraordinarily close affinity. Physically no two men could have been more unlike. Buxton, with his six feet four, towered over his fellows and had been nicknamed Elephant Buxton by his school friends. Wilberforce, small, slight and stooping, had been described by Boswell as a 'shrimp.' But there are many parallels in their lives. Both came to a definite turning point in their spiritual careers. Both had fascination of manner and extraordinary capacity for inspiring affection. Both possessed unshakable determination and unusual powers of concentration and hard work and they spared neither themselves nor others in the cause. Pitt chaffed Wilberforce about 'his white negroes,' while Buxton said that he did 'not care how many white slaves I make so long as the black ones are released.' Both were brought near to death by their excessive labours. Wilberforce was always delicate.

Buxton had a splendid constitution until, at the early age of forty, he had a fit of apoplexy. He was never afterwards very strong, but regardless of his doctor's warnings he continued to do the work of twenty men. When he was only fifty-five his health failed completely. He died at the age of fifty-nine, but at least he had worked himself to death in a good cause.

The two men trusted each other in everything. Apparently almost [1] all Buxton's letters to Wilberforce have been destroyed, but Wilberforce's letters show how close was their friendship.

In his last letter to Buxton, written on July 14, 1833, only three weeks before his death, he says:

> I always feel that on Sundays I love friends who are fellow Christians much better than on any other. My dear friend, may our Heavenly Father fill you with all joy and peace in believing, and be assured that I remain with every good wish for the temporal and spiritual well-being of yourself and all most dear to you, my dear friend, ever sincerely and affectionately yours, W. WILBERFORCE.

Above all, they were united in their religious faith. Their lives were permeated by the things not seen and they took no step without prayer. Their religious intensity does not appear to have repelled even those far removed from them in general outlook. This was perhaps because both men had not only the supreme merits of charity and sincerity, but also the saving graces of humility and sense of humour. Madame de Staël said of Wilberforce: 'I have always heard he was the most religious, but I now find that he is the wittiest man in England.' Buxton did not possess

[1] I am allowed to publish on page 35 an important letter, the existence of which has only now become known.—J. H.

the polished wit of Wilberforce, who remarked of him that he was 'a man who could hew a statue out of a rock, but not cut faces upon cherry stones.'

If Fowell Buxton was not witty he had a hearty and delightful sense of fun. 'Do it with thy might' is the Buxton motto, and no man ever practised the precept more faithfully, whether in work or play. Born on April 1, 1786, at Castle Hedingham, Essex, he was left fatherless in early boyhood, for his father died in 1792. His widow was left with six young children, of whom Thomas Fowell was the eldest. Mrs. Buxton was a woman of vigorous mind, great strength of character and deep religious feeling. Although she was a Quaker and the daughter of a Quaker, her husband remained a member of the Church of England, and she never tried to bring her children to her persuasion. Her religious and moral influence over them was great and she directed all her energies towards making them vigorous and at the same time unselfish in the service of others. She taught them very early to abhor slavery and the slave trade.

As a small boy Fowell Buxton was not very studious; he loved country life and enjoyed hunting, shooting and fishing under the tuition of 'my Guide, philosopher and friend, Abraham Plaistow,' the gamekeeper, whom he described years afterwards as 'for the first twelve years of my life the dearest friend I had.' At the age of fifteen, after eight uneventful years at Dr. Burney's School, he persuaded his mother to allow him to live at home, where he passed his time in sport and desultory reading. At this critical period in the formation of his character the Gurney family came into his life. Mr. John Gurney, of Earlham Hall, near Norwich, was a widower with eleven children, one of whom, Elizabeth, was afterwards Mrs. Fry. The whole family became the life-long friends of Buxton. He paid them long visits and they awakened in him the wide interests and stimulus towards intellectual tastes which had hitherto lain dormant.

At the age of sixteen he was sent to a tutor at Donnybrook to be prepared for Dublin University, and there he studied to such purpose that after a very distinguished career he carried off its highest honours and was asked to represent Dublin University in Parliament. But he was engaged to be married to Miss Hannah Gurney, and with family responsibilities before him, coupled with the necessity of earning his living, he declined the honour, and was married in 1807 at the age of twenty-one. Many years later he referred to his marriage and his undertaking the cause of the slaves as 'the two chief events in my life.' Nothing could have been more ideally happy than his marriage.

He commenced his business career in Truman's Brewery at Spitalfields, and until 1818, when he entered Parliament, he showed that intensity of application which characterised all his activities. How hard he worked may be gathered from a letter written to his mother in 1808: 'was up at four and do not expect to finish my day's work before midnight.' The marked business capacity which he showed caused the senior partners to entrust him with the difficult task of remodelling the whole management of the brewery. The personal interest which he took in the men under his care led him to arrange to have them taught how to read and write. After ten years of this exceedingly strenuous business life it can be no matter for surprise that he began to long increasingly for a wider sphere of public service, and we find him writing, 'I am sick of having my heart in vats.' And again, 'I want to be living in a higher key, to do some good before I die.' He owed much to the friendship of William Allen, the Quaker philosopher and philanthropist, who initiated him into some of the causes to which his after life was devoted.

He was a notable combination of method and enthusiasm and at the beginning of each year he reviewed his aims. His interests grew. Starting with a Savings Bank for Spitalfields and the London Hospital, by 1820 he had added to his interests the Reform of the Penal Code, the Abolition of Suttee, Prison Reform, the Police, Lotteries, the Abolition of the Slave Trade and the Emancipation of the Slaves. Though his labours in connection with slavery demanded nearly all his time and more than all his strength, his interests never became narrow and he was always a great humanitarian and social reformer. As a friend wrote of him after his death, 'He walked through the world like a man passing through the wards of an hospital and stooping down on all sides to administer help where it was needed. . . . He had a singular power of realising to his own mind distant and unseen suffering and of making it his own.'

His sympathy always led to action. Mrs. Fry had interested him in prison conditions and he was one of the original members of the Society for the Reformation of Prison Discipline. It was founded in 1816, and his name stands in the list of the Committee between two of those with whom he was later to work in the cause of the slaves—Dr. Lushington and Lord Suffield (then the Hon. E. Harbord). Just before entering Parliament it might have been expected that it would be Prison and Penal Reform and not Emancipation that would absorb Buxton's energies, for he writes to his wife of a visit which he made to Newgate Prison, where he

saw four poor creatures who are to be executed on Tuesday next. Poor things, God have mercy on them! The sight of them was sufficient for that day. I felt no further inclination to examine the prison. It has made me long much that my life will not pass quite uselessly.

His first important public speech was a remarkable effort. It was made at a Mansion House meeting in aid of the starving weavers of Spitalfields, and shows how intensely he felt their sufferings. He and his relative, Samuel Hoare, had visited many of them, and had seen, he said, 'a degree, an expanse of distress, utterly beyond my powers to describe.' The eloquence and feeling of his speech made so deep an impression on his audience that a sum of £43,369 was quickly subscribed, towards which the Prince Regent upon reading the speech sent £5,000. It was also the cause of his first contact with Wilberforce, from whom he received a letter prophetic of their future labours together for suffering humanity. Wilberforce wrote, November 20, 1816:

My dear Sir, I must in three words express the real pleasure with which I have both read and heard of your successful effort on Tuesday last in behalf of the hungry and the naked. It is partly a selfish feeling, for I anticipate the success of the efforts which I trust you will one day make in other instances, in an assembly in which I trust we shall be fellow labourers, both in the motives by which we are actuated, and in the objects to which our exertions will be directed.

Both men indeed had the powerful instinct for philanthropy of the 'Anima naturaliter Christiana.'

For some time, Buxton's predominating human interests were in the poor and in questions connected with crime, punishment and prison reform. Early in 1818 he published 'An Inquiry whether Crime be produced or prevented by our Present System of Prison Discipline.' It attracted wide attention and was highly praised in the House of Commons by Sir James Mackintosh, later one of Buxton's fellow workers in the Emancipation of the Slaves. Again Wilberforce wrote to him, and after congratulating him on the weight which his work appeared to carry he added:

may it please God to continue to animate you with as much benevolent zeal and to direct it to worthy objects. I hope you will come soon into Parliament and be able to contend in person, as well as with your pen, for the rights and happiness of the oppressed and the friendless. I claim you as an ally in this blessed league.

Wilberforce had not long to wait, for Buxton entered Parliament in 1818 as Member for Weymouth. In politics, though nominally a Whig, he, like Wilberforce, was from the beginning independent of party ties. When his Dublin University friend, John Henry North, thought of entering Parliament (as a Tory) Buxton urged him to stand and described his own attitude in the following words:

My line is distinctly drawn, I care but little about Party politics—I vote as I like . . . but I feel the greatest interest in subjects such as the Slave Trade, the condition of the poor, Prisons and Criminal Law; to these I devote myself and should be quite content never to give another vote upon a party question.

Although Wilberforce had yet fifteen years to live, he was deeply conscious of his own physical frailty. During three years after Buxton took his seat, the two men became still more closely wedded to each other's purposes. They thought alike, they shared the same ideas and they reciprocated each other's deep religious experiences. Wilberforce felt that at last the time had come to throw his mantle over Buxton, and on May 24, 1821, he wrote to him:

Now for many years, I have been longing to bring forward that great subject, the condition of the Negro Slaves in our Trans-Atlantic Colonies; and the best means of providing for their moral and social improvement; and ultimately for their advancement to the rank of a free peasantry. A Cause this, commended to me or rather enforced on me by every consideration of Religion, Justice and Humanity. I have been waiting with no little solicitude for a proper time and suitable circumstances of the country for introducing this great business, and of late for some Member of Parliament, who, if I were to retire, or to be laid by, would be an eligible leader in this Holy Enterprise. I have for some time been viewing you in this connection and after what passed last night I can no longer forbear writing to you, as I formerly did to Pitt, and earnestly conjuring you to take most seriously into consideration the expediency of your devoting yourself to this *Blessed Service*.

Buxton was one who undertook nothing lightly. He felt the tremendous responsibility of consenting to take up the burden from Wilberforce, and it was not until eighteen months after receiving the latter's appeal that he decided finally to undertake the great task of

Emancipation. Other influences had joined with that of Wilberforce. His brother-in-law, William Forster, urged the claims of Emancipation upon him: so did the Gurneys, and it was during this year that, as we have already seen, Priscilla Gurney died, begging him, with her last breath, to remember the slaves.

By the autumn of 1822 his mind was made up. Wilberforce, Zachary Macaulay, Dr. Lushington and Lord Suffield joined him at Cromer Hall. 'Long and deep were their deliberations, how best to shape those measures which were to change the structure of Society throughout the Western World.'[1] Nothing could have been closer than the friendship between this band of brothers, all animated by the same ideals. Earl Buxton has well described them: 'Wilberforce was his Nestor. Zachary Macaulay, who had been an active lieutenant to Wilberforce in the campaign against the slave trade, was described by Buxton in 1833 as "the real leader of this Cause, the Anti-Slavery tutor of us all." Dr. Lushington, who avoided the limelight, was admirable in counsel and a partner in every idea and every plan. Lord Brougham, who delighted in publicity, was an enthusiastic supporter; J. J. Gurney (Buxton's brother-in-law), Lord Suffield, James Stephen, Sir James Mackintosh, O'Connell, and others rendered yeoman service.' Mr. Denman was another stalwart.

In Parliament they were indeed few. In a private conversation in 1841 Buxton, looking back over the struggle for Emancipation, said:

For several years there were only six of us in the House, Sykes, Wm. Smith, Wm. Evans, Dr. Lushington, myself and

[1] *Life of Wilberforce*, v, 160.

Brougham. . . . Wilberforce also occasionally aided at first, but was soon obliged to give up. Constantly we were completely done up for want of speakers. I remember a whole array of West Indians sitting opposite to us, while of our own party, there were only Dr. Lushington and I. We were always anxious not to appear so few, so he and I agreed each to make speeches, and the others applaud, which we did. . . . We were tired of always speaking, and had, on coming into the House, to apply to Evans, who, though the honestest fellow in the world . . . when unprepared, made atrocious ones [speeches]; however, that time he got on pretty well.

Of Lushington, Buxton said: 'He has ever been as disinterested, as honest, as generous a supporter of our great Cause as could be.' Every idea, every plan, was arranged between them, but not one-tenth part of Lushington's work ever met the public eye.

Mr. Charles Buxton, in the memoir of his father, has left us a vivid picture of Zachary Macaulay:

Mr. Macaulay's stooping figure, his entangled utterance and neglected dress—but within there dwelt the spirit of a hero and a heart glowing with love to God and man. From the moment of his embracing the abolition cause till the day of his death, he flinched neither from toil nor privations, neither from obloquy or persecution, but sacrificed himself, with the whole of his personal hopes, to advancing the cause of humanity.

Of this group, Buxton's striking qualities of character, his integrity and single-mindedness, iron determination coupled with sound judgment, made him the unquestioned leader. He was always distinguished by balance. His moderation, indeed, got him into hot water on more than one occasion with the more ardent of his supporters. But his judgment was seldom at fault, and if it proved to be so he was the first to acknowledge it. He could be dogged to the last degree, but with all his strength he was the most patient of men and he never showed a trace of bitterness. The foundations both of his strength and his serenity were in his Christian faith, his ideally happy home life and his love of nature.

After an exhausting fight in Parliament he loved to escape to 'the peace, the divine peace, of the country.' He took great delight in his horses and dogs and had all the Buxton love of birds and of nature. He was a devoted father, and even when overwhelmed with Parliamentary work found time to write to his little boys about their ponies and what they would do in the world when they grew up. They were never afraid to come to him. His manner to them as they grew older is shown in a letter written by one of his sons, then a mere boy:

> I cannot help being struck with the exquisite tenderness of heart which my father always displays; his unwillingness to debar us from pleasure, the zeal with which he will make any sacrifice or take any trouble to gratify us, is most surprising. One little example to-day will describe his whole conduct. He, being really unwell, was lying nearly asleep on the sofa and observing me upon another with my feet hanging over the side, he quietly got up, placed a chair under them, and then lay down again. His whole appearance with his worn and thoughtful face, is so much that of a man whom one would approach with some sensation of awe, that these small, though exquisite acts of tenderness are the more unexpected and consequently the more pleasing.

One of his maxims was: 'Let it be your first duty to teach the world that you are not wood and straw—*some iron in you.*' Of his eight children, the eldest, a boy of ten years old, died in 1820, and less than five weeks afterwards three little girls died also, of measles. Eleven years later, his second boy, Harry, died after a long illness. What these losses must have meant to a family so happy and united can be imagined. Wilberforce understood, for he and his wife had suffered like losses.

Buxton's religion was his rock, his strength and his comfort. The Rev. J. W. Cunningham refers to 'the child-like simplicity of his faith.' He and some of his friends met every night when the House was sitting to pray and read the Bible and he was very often the 'Chaplain.' He was a loyal member of the Church of England, but was entirely free from sectarianism. Through his mother, his wife, the Gurneys, William Allen and others he was all his life in very close touch with the Society of Friends and found help and comfort in their quiet meetings, besides invaluable support for the Anti-Slavery Cause. His attitude is well illustrated in a letter to his brother-in-law, Andrew Johnston, in 1839:

> Yesterday I was whipt off to a meeting in the city on the subject of Bethnal Green, and had to tell the Bishop of London that I was ready to join Methodists or Baptists, or Quakers, or any honest body, in spreading Christianity in Bethnal Green; but he took it very kindly.

He was glad and thankful to work with *all* Christians in *all* good causes.

Soon after entering Parliament, Fowell Buxton took part in debates on the subject of Convict Transport, but it was not until March, 1819, that he made his first big speech in seconding Sir James Mackintosh's motion for the Reform of the Criminal Code. Buxton had studied the question thoroughly and his sterling good sense, his good language and his earnest manner made an extremely favourable impression on the House. Select Committees were set up for the Reform of the Penal Code and of Prison Discipline. He served on both Committees and the resultant reforms fully repaid him and Sir James Mackintosh for their labours.

It may be well at this stage to take a bird's-eye view of the whole question in order to see how each stage led to the next. Many of the early Abolitionists, indeed, had little or no thought of the Emancipation of the Slaves. Clarkson, who had worked with Wilberforce from the first, expressed and described his own attitude and that of Wilberforce in a letter to Buxton: 'When my dear and revered friend, Mr. Wilberforce and others first embarked on it, we directed our endeavours as a first step, to the Abolition of the Slave Trade only. . . . But you, who succeed us, take a wider field of labour.' Abolition in 1807, led to Emancipation in 1833. Thereafter Britain, in the strength of a clear conscience, warred ceaselessly against the Slave Trade still carried on by foreign countries. By degrees not the Slave Trade only, but Slave-owning itself, was made illegal in the possessions of the more civilised countries. Finally, in our own day, the League of Nations has taken in hand 'the abolition of Slavery in all its forms,' and put into words the great principle of Trusteeship. But that principle had been grasped by Buxton many years before. To his far-sightedness, vision and wide grasp, not only of immediate objectives but of ultimate aims, belongs a greater share of the credit for the ultimate transformation of British public opinion from the acceptance of slavery to the ideal of Trusteeship than even we, who to-day see the whole picture in perspective, are perhaps capable of realising. He grasped not only the principles but the practice of Trusteeship. He realised that newly freed slaves could not at once stand alone, but he trusted them and believed in giving them responsibility.

His advocacy of international action against the Slave Trade, on the lines which the League of Nations is only now beginning to adopt, was many years ahead of his time. So was his clear understanding of the fundamental importance to the native of the land and labour questions.

CHAPTER III

Abolitionists and Emancipators

'They conquer who believe they can.'

Motion for Emancipation—Attitude of Canning—Conflict between Planters and Colonial Office—Wilberforce applies for Chiltern Hundreds—Slaves' Revolt—Slave Trade in Mauritius—The Hottentots of South Africa—The Decision of 1830—The Cruelties of Slavery—The 1832 Insurrection—The Emancipation Bill—Victory—Death of Wilberforce.

It was not until sixteen years after the Abolition of Slave-trading, namely in 1823, that operations against Slave-owning were commenced with vigour. In March Wilberforce published his well-known 'Appeal on behalf of the Slaves.' The Anti-Slavery Committee was formed, with Buxton as one of its Vice-Presidents. In Parliament, Wilberforce presented a petition against Slavery from the Society of Friends. Canning asked whether it was his intention to found any motion upon it. Wilberforce said that it was not, but that such was the intention of an esteemed friend.

On May 15, 1823, Buxton launched the Parliamentary campaign by moving

that the state of Slavery is repugnant to the principles of the British Constitution and of the Christian religion; and that it ought to be gradually abolished throughout the British Colonies with as much expedition as may be found consistent with a due regard to the well-being of the parties concerned.

In his speech he declared plainly that

the object at which we aim is nothing less than the extinction of slavery—in nothing less than the whole of the British dominions; not, however, the rapid termination of that state; not the sudden emancipation of the negro, but such preparatory steps, such measures of precaution, as, by slow degrees, and in a course of years, first ntting and qualifying the slaves for the enjoyment of freedom, shall gently conduct us to the annihilation of Slavery.

These words are enough to refute the charge brought against the Emancipators of wishing to give the slaves freedom before they were fit for it. It was the planters who persisted in rejecting all preparatory measures because they were meant to pave the way to emancipation. Buxton urged as a first and immediate step the emancipation of the children of the slaves, pointing out how surely, though slowly, slavery would thus die out. In a remarkable passage he dealt with the right of the master:

There are persons whose notions of justice are so confused and confounded by slavery, as to suppose that the planter has something like an honest title to the person of the slave. We have been so long accustomed to talk of 'my slave' and 'your slave,' and what he will fetch, if sold, that we are apt to imagine that he is really *yours* or *mine*, and, that we have a substantial right to keep or sell him. Then let us just for a moment fathom this right. Here is a certain valuable commodity, and here are two claimants for it, a white man and a black man. Now, what is the commodity in dispute? The body of the black man. The white man says, 'it is mine,' and the black man, 'it is mine.' Now the question is, if every man had his own, to whom would the black body belong? The claim of the black man is just this. Nature gave it to him. He holds it by the grant of God. . . . At least you will admit this. The negro has a pretty good prima facie claim to his own person. If any man thinks he has a better, the onus probandi rests with him. Then we come to the claim of the white man. What is the foundation of your right? It shall be the best that can possibly be conceived. You received him from your father—very good. Your father bought him from a neighbouring planter—very good. That planter bought him of a trader in the Kingston Slave Market, and that trader bought him of a man merchant in Africa—so far you are quite safe!

How did the man merchant acquire him? *He stole him*, he kidnapped him, the very root of your claim is robbery, violence, inconceivable wickedness. If anything was ever proved by evidence, it was proved by the Slave Trade Committee that the method of obtaining slaves in Africa was robbery, man-stealing and murder. Your pure title rests on these sacred foundations. If your slave came direct from Africa, your right to his person is absolutely nothing. But your claim to the child born in Jamaica is (if I may use the expression) less still. The new-born infant has done, can have done, nothing to forfeit his right to freedom. And to talk about rights, justice, equity and law as connected with slavery, is downright nonsense.

Canning, for the Government, replied sympathetically but was greatly afraid of the difficulties of Emancipation. The Resolutions moved and carried by Canning declared that it was 'expedient to adopt effectual and decisive measures for ameliorating the condition of the population in His Majesty's Indies,' that H.M. Government looked 'forward to a progressive improvement in the character of the slave population, such as may prepare them for a participation in those civil rights and privileges which are enjoyed by other classes of His Majesty's subjects,' and

> That this House is anxious for the accomplishment of this purpose, at the earliest period that shall be compatible with the interest of the slaves themselves, with the safety of the Colonies and with a fair and equitable consideration of the rights of private property.

Buxton's reply at the conclusion of the debate was, according to Wilberforce, 'short and, not sweet indeed; but excellent.' In replying to the argument that to discuss slavery in the House would make the negroes discontented he exclaimed :

> What then, does the slave require any hint from us that he is a slave and that slavery is of all conditions the most miserable ? Why, Sir, he hears this, he sees it, he feels it, too, in all around him. He sees his harsh uncompensated labour ; he hears the crack of the whip ; he feels—he writhes under the lash. . . . He sees the mother of his children stripped naked before the gang of male negroes and flogged unmercifully ; he sees his children sent to market, to be sold at the best price they will fetch ; he sees in himself not a man, but a thing ; . . . will any man tell me [exclaimed Buxton], that the negro, with all this staring him in the face, never dreams there is injustice in such treatment till he sits down to the perusal of an English newspaper, and there, to his astonishment, discovers that there are enthusiasts in England who from the bottom of their hearts deplore and abhor all negro slavery ? There are such enthusiasts ; I am one of them ; and while we breathe, we will never abandon the cause, till that thing—that chattel—is reinstated in all the privileges of man !

The immediate practical result of Buxton's Motion was that letters were addressed by the Government to the various Colonial authorities, *recommending* (but only *recommending*) reforms which included religious instruction for the slaves, prohibition of Sunday labour, legalisation of marriage, prevention of separation of families by sale or otherwise, restraint of the master's power of arbitrary punishment, abolition of the driving whip in the field, abolition of 'the degrading corporal punishment of females,' and admission of the evidence of the slaves in Court of Justice. This last was an important point, for, as Wilberforce wrote to Buxton (1826), 'Where black witnesses cannot give evidence in a case which affects the life of a white man, the law is an absolute premium on murder.'

'Those canting hypocritical rascals,' as the Emancipators were called by the *Jamaica Journal* in June, 1828, had difficult days before them. When the Home Government's Order in Council recommending reforms reached Demerara, the authorities stupidly tried to conceal the news from the negroes, with the result that the slaves believed that 'the great King of England' had set them free and that the planters had suppressed the Edict. On several estates they refused to work. Compulsion was resorted to, they resisted, and the troops were called out. Not one soldier was killed, but pressed down and running over was the vengeance meted out to the unhappy slaves. As Brougham said in Parliament, 'It was deemed fitting to make tremendous examples of them,' and he described the executions of prisoners and how 'within the short space of a week ten were torn to pieces by the lash; some of these had been condemned to six or seven hundred lashes, five to one thousand each; of which inhuman torture one had received the whole, and the others almost the whole at once.'

The West Indian planters took vengeance not only

on the slaves but on the missionaries, and when the revolt took place they resolved to fix the blame upon the Independent and Wesleyan missionaries. Many were persecuted and a missionary named John Smith was tried in an illegal manner before a court-martial of officers and condemned to be hanged; but his treatment in prison had destroyed his already failing health and he anticipated the executioner by dying in his dungeon.

The Emancipators in England were bitterly blamed for the revolt and for the colonists' anger and discontent. Worse still, the Government took fright at the colonial protests and weakened so perceptibly that Buxton arranged an interview with Canning, when his worst fears were confirmed, for he writes Feb. 14, 1823: 'We have had a very unsatisfactory interview with Canning. The Government mean to *forfeit their pledge* and do next to nothing.' Three days later Buxton, now almost despairing, writes: 'The Slavery question looks wretchedly. I begin to think that, opposed as we are by the West Indians, deserted by Government, and deemed enthusiasts by the public, we shall be able to do little or nothing. However, I rejoice that we have tried.' Ridicule and abuse were now heaped upon the Emancipators. They were stigmatised as fools, or knaves, or both. When the storm was at its height, one of Buxton's friends asked him what he was to say when he heard him attacked. 'Say,' he replied, snapping his fingers, 'Say that! You good folk think too much of your good name. Do right, and right will be done you.'

The Government [wrote Buxton] have determined to yield to the West Indian clamour and do nothing, except in Trinidad, where there is no Colonial Assembly . . . this timidity is very painful. It frustrates all our hopes and it will enable the West Indians to say that we are wild enthusiastic people, and that the people of England ought to be guided by the sober discretion of Government—which sober discretion is downright timidity.

Canning, speaking for the Government, carefully withdrew his support from the Emancipators, whom he now discovered to be acting 'under the impulses of enthusiasm.' Buxton had been pressed, even by some of his own followers, to receive the attack in silence. But he was at all times a bold leader and he at once dauntlessly attacked the Government for its vacillation. He concluded his speech, in which he described atrocious cruelties inflicted on the negroes, by stating :

No man is more aware than I am of my inability to follow the brilliant and able speech which has just been delivered [Canning]. But I have a duty to perform and I will perform it. I know well what I incur by this. . . . I have no hostility to the planter. Compensation to the planter, emancipation to the children of the negro—these are my desires, this is the consummation, the just and glorious consummation, on which my hopes are planted, and to which, as long as I live, my most strenuous efforts shall be directed.

Lushington, Evans and Wilberforce supported him vigorously.

Wilberforce wrote to him after the debate that, despite appearances, he could discern

streaks of morning light. I hope I may live to congratulate you, even in this world, upon the complete success of your generous labours—at all events, I trust humbly that we may rejoice and triumph together in a better world, for we, my dear friend, may, more truly than the great historian, affirm that we are working for eternity.

Brougham's powerful speech in the following June, on a motion respecting the missionary, John Smith, produced a deep effect on public opinion. The nation, which had shared the alarm and timidity of the Government, began to awaken to the real nature of the crime of slavery. It was at this juncture that Denman joined the little band of Emancipators in the House of Commons.

After a continuous Parliamentary career of forty-one years, Wilberforce was compelled by ill-health to retire early in 1825, and he entrusted his friend with the task of applying on his behalf for the Chiltern Hundreds.

I should like you [wrote Wilberforce] to be the person to move for a new writ for Bramber as my Parliamentary Executor. I can now only say, may God bless you and yours, bless you in public and private. . . . So wishes, so prays for you and all that are most dear to you—Your ever sincere and affectionate friend, W. Wilberforce.

The hitherto unpublished letter which we print here shows how deeply Buxton esteemed the honour.

Cromer Hall,
Feby. 6, 1825.

My dear Friend,

I fully expected that the time was not far distant in which you could come to the conclusion that you ought to quit Parlt., and yet in spite of this degree of preparation your letter has made me feel thoroughly melancholy.—Not however that I by any means question the propriety of your resolutions. —Your life is eminently important not merely to your family and friends but to many great causes—and therefore I confess that it is good economy to avoid the risk of Parliamentary honors,—&c. &c.

The Carthaginians put upon Hannibal's tomb 'We vehemently desired him in the day of battle,' which exactly describes my feelings—I go to town to-morrow by Mail—and therefore shall arrive there as soon as this does—I shall see you as early as possible. I need not say I feel it an honour to be ranked among the numbers of your friends—and to be known as resolved to devote myself to some of those subjects which have been under your care. So far as I am flattered and gratified by the proposal of moving for the new writ—on the other hand there is not, I am sure, one particle of affectation in the declaration that I feel myself in every respect totally unworthy and incompetent to represent you—With my best regards to Mrs. W. and your daughter,

Yours very truly,
T. F. BUXTON.

During these first years of the struggle for Emancipation success seemed far distant, and the main task of the Anti-Slavery leaders was by investigation and exposure of the evils and cruelties of the system to prepare the way. They owed much to that 'mighty book,' as they called it, 'Delineation of Slavery,' by the veteran opponent of the Slave Trade, James Stephen.

In 1825 Buxton exposed in Parliament the treatment meted out by the planters to Mr. Shrewsbury, a Wesleyan missionary in Barbados, who, for instructing and preaching the Gospel to the negroes and for no other crime, had his Chapel and Mission House pulled down by an infuriated mob, and his life attempted. At the end of the debate the House was content to pass a vote of censure on those concerned in the crime. Again Buxton showed his genius for leadership by seizing upon the real issues at stake, pressing home the cruelty and crime of slavery, and ending his speech with these words: 'I wish it to be clearly understood that it is my firm and unalterable resolution to devote all my life to the cause of the slaves and that I will persist in that cause in spite of opposition, unpopularity, obloquy or falsehood.'

In 1826 Denman entered the lists by raising the question of the illegality of the death sentence on eight of the negroes executed after the Jamaica insurrection. The House resolved that it would be inexpedient to impeach the sentences which had been already carried out, but 'that further proof had been afforded by them of the evils inseparably attendant upon a state of slavery.' The latter part of this Resolution was striking evidence of the effect which the growth of public opinion was having upon Parliament. The dogged determination of the Emancipators was doing its work both in the House and outside it. During the years 1826–27, the period of grace which had been granted by Canning to the Colonial authorities, the Emancipators had perforce to hold their hand.

Buxton, however, was making good use of the time by prosecuting enquiries into what proved to be an outrageous state of affairs in Mauritius. Mr. Byam, late Commissary General of Police in that island, gave Buxton first-hand evidence that in spite of the prohibition of 1807, slave-trading on a large scale was openly carried on with the island and that atrocious cruelties were being inflicted on the slaves. James Stephen undertook the task of collecting further evidence, and in May, 1826, Buxton brought the question before Parliament. He described in detail the horrors, first of the capture of the slaves in Africa, and then of their fourteen hundred mile voyage to Mauritius, packed 'until, to use the expression of an eye-witness, "they are wedged together in one mass of living corruption."' His charges were so well supported by facts that he obtained, without much difficulty, a Select Committee to enquire whether the Slave Trade existed in Mauritius.

A year later, in May, 1827, Buxton was violently attacked by the late Governor of the island, Sir Robert Farquhar, who challenged him to prove his statements. This challenge came at a time when Buxton was seriously overworked and unwell, and he wrote to a friend, 'Ought I to overwork myself, or underwork my slave cause?' He spent May 19 in making a survey of the evidence of the atrocious cruelties practised upon the negroes in Mauritius. Several times he exclaimed aloud, entirely overcome by his feelings, 'Oh, it's too bad! I can't bear it.' Next morning he had a fit of apoplexy and was unconscious for several days. His first words on regaining consciousness were that he must go to the House and bring forward his Motion on Mauritius.

But the appointed day had passed and the motion had been dropped. For over a year Fowell Buxton's health remained very precarious and sustained exertion was impossible. On March 6, 1828, Mr. Wilmot Horton, a leading West Indian, brought forward a reactionary motion [1] opposing manumission, which the Emancipators were bound to challenge. Buxton had been too unwell to study the documents and went down to the House with no intention of speaking, where he found himself the only member of his group present, with the exception of William Smith, who was by no means a powerful speaker. It was in these

[1] See Hansard, March 6, 1828.

circumstances, unprepared, ill, and almost alone, but spiritually aflame, that he made what was not only one of the noblest but one of the ablest and most forcible speeches of his life. One of his friends wrote afterwards: 'The whole House was carried along by his earnestness, cheered him vehemently and listened attentively.'

Lushington and Brougham had for some time been at work on behalf of the free people of colour and in 1828 their efforts were completely successful. An Order in Council was issued by which they were placed at once on the same footing as Europeans; a measure whose happy consequences to the whole future of the West Indies are to be seen to this day.

Buxton had barely carried through his great work for Mauritius when his help was sought for the Hottentots of South Africa. Here his efforts were crowned with easy and complete success. Briefed by Dr. Philip, of the London Missionary Society, Buxton proved that the Hottentots, though not the legal property of individuals, were 'practically slaves,' that their rich lands and vast herds of cattle were the prey of the Dutch and English settlers and that they themselves were at the mercy of all who chose to oppress them or to compel them to work. Sir George Murray, then Colonial Secretary, accepted Buxton's Motion, and an Order in Council was sent out to the Cape. From that day onwards the Hottentots were entirely emancipated, protected by the same laws as the white man, permitted to own property, to demand wages, and no longer tied to their villages. With the help of the missionaries they made rapid progress. The Kat River Settlement was founded for them by the Cape

Government, and so early as 1832, only four years after Buxton's successful effort on their behalf, it is stated that 'the success of the Hottentots has been equal to their industry, and good conduct. By patient labour, with manly moderation and Christian temperance, they have converted the desert into a fruitful field.' Buxton 'thanked God' that he had been 'entrusted with this easy and honourable task.'

During 1829 Parliament was chiefly occupied with the question of Catholic Emancipation. Buxton voted for it, though sure that it would cost him his seat, for the Weymouth electors were strongly opposed to it, but in his opinion 'the peace and safety of Ireland depend upon our vote.'

The Government now decided to appoint Protectors of Slaves for the four Crown Colonies, and Buxton persuaded Mr. John Jeremie, late Chief Justice of St. Lucia, who had incurred the hatred of the planters there by his abhorrence of the cruelty with which the slaves were treated, to undertake the office of Protector of the Slaves in Mauritius. When the proposal was first made to Jeremie he said that he had already suffered enough. 'Why,' said Buxton, 'it signifies very little whether you are killed or not: but it signifies very much whether the right man goes to Mauritius.' Jeremie went. His life was repeatedly threatened and even attempted. He was insulted, abused, harassed at every turn, and eventually recalled, but the incident illustrates not only his own courage and determination, but Buxton's power of inspiring these qualities in others.

In 1830 the Abolitionists took a vital decision. For seven years they had pursued a policy of persuading

Government and Colonists to bring about Emancipation by evolution. Buxton had moved in 1823 for the first gradual steps to be taken towards 'fitting the Slaves for the enjoyment of freedom,' but in 1830 he, with the other leaders, had come to recognise that 'all attempts at gradual evolution are wild and visionary.' It was only too clear that the planters were violently opposed to all reform. The new policy was launched in the Freemasons' Hall in May, 1830. Wilberforce was in the chair and Buxton proposed 'at the earliest period the entire abolition of Slavery throughout the British dominions.' This was carried with great enthusiasm. Public opinion was indeed aroused, but the Government had no desire to accelerate the pace. Thus Buxton was wrestling now not so much with the West Indians as with a reluctant Government. In July Brougham succeeded in obtaining a large minority in favour of ultimate Emancipation and by November Buxton was more hopeful:

> Our Slavery concerns go on well [he wrote]: the religious public has, at last, taken the field. The West Indians have done us good service. They have of late flogged slaves in Jamaica for praying and imprisoned the missionaries and they have given the nation to understand that preaching and praying are offences not to be tolerated in a slave colony. That is right—it exhibits slavery in its true colours—it enforces your doctrine, that, if you wish to teach religion to slaves, the first thing is, to put down slavery.

In every speech Buxton and his colleagues gave careful and exact evidence of the sufferings of the slaves—and it is essential that their sufferings should be realised. It is not suggested that all masters were inhuman, but that slavery itself is a system which only too often 'makes of the slaves brutes and the masters devils.' The master had almost absolute power, and public opinion was invariably on his side, even in a case so revolting as that charged against Mr. and Mrs. Moss, who were tried in the Bahama Courts in 1826 for fatal cruelty to their slave Kate. Accused of disobedience and of refusing to mend her clothes, she was confined in the stocks for seventeen days, flogged six times during that period, and sent to field labour. When she complained of cramp and fever, she was flogged again twice in three days, and the official report concludes, 'in the morning at 7 o'clock she was taken to work in the field, where she died at noon.' Mr. and Mrs. Moss were sentenced to five months' imprisonment and a fine of £300. 'The most respectable people of the island petitioned for a mitigation of their punishment, and finally, on their liberation from jail, gave them a public dinner.' To us at this period of history, the cruelty and degradation of the slavery imposed by white men seem well-nigh incredible. The bodies of the slaves were torn to pieces by the cruel lash. A South African judge has stated that 10 lashes is about as many as the body can stand, but in the West Indies punishments of 50 to 100 lashes were sometimes inflicted, and there are even cases recorded of 1,000 lashes. Elsewhere we read of slaves who were broken on the wheel, crucified, tortured. Gelding was a common practice. The immorality involved in slavery was one of its most serious evils. The juxtaposition of female slaves on the one hand and planters and overseers on the other, led to inevitable and flagrant moral evils. The slave could not even call his wife his own or protect his daughter.

The Barbados Legislature in 1826 decided that 'to forbid by legislative enactment the flogging of female slaves would, in the judgment of the Assembly, be productive of the most injurious consequences. The power of inflicting summary punishment, by the whip, the Assembly considers to be inseparable from a state of slavery.'

The instrument of punishment was the heavy leather cartwhip, capable of cutting deeply into the flesh. Dr. Williamson (though himself an advocate of the Colonial system) observed: 'If, in a warm day, we pass by a gang when they are uncovered, it is a shame to every white man to observe in them the recently lacerated sores, or the deep furrows which, though healed up, leave the marks of cruel punishment.' Many of the worst abuses arose from the fact that the wealthier proprietors lived in England and left their estates under the control of overseers who committed cruelties of which the owners had no knowledge. The total number of floggings was appalling. Official records show that in the four Crown Colonies of Demerara, Berbice, St. Lucia and Trinidad (in which, owing to the power of the Crown, slavery existed in its mildest form), 68,921 punishments, of which 25,094 were upon women, were registered in the two years 1828–29. The legal limit of 25 stripes was frequently exceeded. Estimating only 20 lashes per punishment, the number of lashes inflicted reaches the enormous total, in these four islands in two years, of not less than 1,350,000 lashes.[1]

[1] Large numbers of punishments were unregistered—*e.g.*, in Demerara, in 1829: 'Mary Lowe, convicted of tying up first a little girl and then a little boy, by the wrists, the one

The whip was only one of many forms of cruelty. The feeding of the slaves was always poor and often insufficient, particularly when their long hours of exhausting work under a blazing sun are considered. In Jamaica the legally permitted hours were 19 hours a day during crop time and 14½ during the remainder of the year (with intervals of rest amounting to 2½ hours).

'The slaves were divided into gangs of from 30 to 50 persons . . . they were placed in a line in the field, with drivers (armed with the whip) at equal distances . . . those who were not so strong as the others were literally flogged up by the drivers.' No wonder that the slave population declined.

In one of Buxton's most effective and important speeches in the House (April 15, 1831), he gave statistics proving that 'in the last ten years the slave population in those fourteen colonies had decreased by 45,800 persons.' The appalling fact was never denied that between the Abolition of the Slave Trade in 1807 and 1830, the slave population of the West Indies had, in spite of importations, decreased from 800,000 to 700,000. Buxton went on to say, 'the fact is that the whip extorts from the slave a degree of physical exertion which the human constitution cannot support. Terrible accounts (of cruelties) have been received in England within this day or two. The whip, however, is not the cause of mortality. *It is extreme toil.*'

He showed that in contrast to the terrible decrease among the West Indian slaves, the free negroes of Hayti had more than doubled their numbers in twenty

---

for 5, the other for 9 hours, and flogging them unmercifully, and of other cruelties.' Yet her estate gave no returns of punishments. See Parliamentary Returns.

years. He concluded by moving a Resolution to the effect that slavery 'should be dealt with, not by palliatives, but by destroying it altogether,' and that the House should 'adopt the best means of effecting its abolition throughout the British dominions.' Lord Althorp, replying for the Government, refused to accept the Motion but thought it time 'to adopt other measures with the Colonists than those of mere recommendations.' The debate was adjourned, but O'Connell, who throughout gave steady and energetic support, came across the floor of the House and said, 'Buxton, I see land.'

The year 1832 opened with an insurrection in Jamaica. As in Demerara in 1828, the negroes thought that 'the free paper was come' and was being suppressed by the planters. Many were shot. The planters again tried to implicate the missionaries, two of whom, Gardner and Knibb, were arrested, but not one tittle of evidence could be brought against them and the charge broke down.

At home the West Indian proprietors and their friends in the House of Lords obtained a Committee of Inquiry on West Indian affairs. Buxton feared it would mean delay, for Suffield was almost the only consistent supporter of Emancipation among the temporal peers. He wrote to Suffield (April 19, 1832): 'I could hardly listen to them (the Lords) in silence the other night, or refrain from cheering the solitary voice that was lifted up for truth and righteousness. . . . I cannot but congratulate you on what I consider so pre-eminently the post of honour.' A few days later, when Suffield was dispirited, Buxton wrote to him again: 'Away with all mortification. I can truly say, that I would rather incur obloquy, shame and disappointment in our good cause, than get glory in any other; and I know nothing of your mind if you are not of the same opinion.' Buxton prepared his evidence for the Lords' Committee with great care, and although its Report was indecisive, the evidence did much to educate the Peers.

In the country the feeling grew daily stronger. The passage of the Reform Bill in 1832 and the General Election which followed it gave the Emancipators a great accession of strength in Parliament. During the Election, 'All the way through, instead of Corn laws or anything else Slavery was the cry.'[1] Many members had pledged themselves to support Emancipation, and with his hands thus strengthened Buxton determined to bring Parliament to a decision. Not that his task was easy, for, as he wrote, even the 'select band of our special friends and faithful supporters differed upon every practical point.' His daughter wrote: 'We are almost in a fight at the Anti-Slavery Parliament, as it is called. . . . Papa says that people's principles are the greatest nuisance in life. How he will ever manage his 250 refractory horses and get them to pull all one way is quite beyond my power to think.'

Nevertheless, greatly as Buxton's supporters in the new House differed on practical and important points such as compensation to the planters and instant or gradual Abolition, they were at one in their condemnation of Slavery, and Buxton was undoubtedly right in feeling that the moment had come to demand immediate Emancipation. Accordingly, he gave notice

[1] Letter from Buxton's daughter quoting a Candidate.

of a Motion. The Government were afraid of dividing their own supporters. The utmost pressure was brought to bear on him, even by his own friends. But he was now a seasoned Parliamentarian of fourteen years' standing, and he was above all a leader who knew his subject, his followers and his public. He stood firm. The cruelty of slavery was established beyond question. Persuasion had been tried with the planters and had failed; the state of the slaves was not one whit better. The only remedy was to end the system. His daughter describes how at this time he met with every possible opposition from friend and foe in the vain attempt to persuade him to postpone his Motion, and when that was found hopeless, to induce him to tone it down, or not to divide the House. Even Lushington was persuaded to counsel delay. 'Nearly every friend he had in the House came to him and . . . besought him to give way.'

Buxton, instinctively seeing victory ahead of boldness, gave to all of them a resolute 'no,' though, he says, 'I found it very difficult to stand firm. I felt far more distressed than I ought to have done at acting in hostility to my friends.'

His Motion was of course defeated, but in spite of the abstention of many who ought to have supported him, he obtained an unexpectedly large measure of support against the Government's proposals for delay, and drew from Althorp the remark: 'That Division of Buxton's has settled the Slavery question. If he can get 90 to vote with him when he is wrong, and when most of those really interested in the question vote against him, he can command a majority when he is right. The question is settled'—and it was!

Buxton himself said of this debate, 'the Cause made a seven league stride.' He had need of all his fortitude, for he was being at the same time furiously attacked by the more ardent section of the Anti-Slavery party for his moderation. Joseph Sturge was amongst his critics, but Buxton always appreciated and valued the zeal of which these criticisms were evidence. His attitude is defined in a letter to Zachary Macaulay, December, 1832:

> Immediate and total emancipation is our right, and if we yield an iota of it, it must not be for the sake of the planter, nor for the sake of the Government, but for the benefit of the negro; and we must give up no more than it is in the interest of the negro to surrender. In short, we must fight the battle with a single eye to the benefit of our clients, the slaves.

The year of Victory, 1833, opened with an appeal from Buxton to the Churches to set aside January 16 as a day of prayer on the subject of slavery. In his own prayers it was never forgotten: 'Oh, give these unhappy creatures their liberty—and that liberty in peace, and protect their masters from ruin and desolation.'

It was understood that Earl Grey's Government had decided definitely to bring in an Emancipation Bill. Great was the disappointment of the Abolitionists when the King's Speech made no mention of the subject. Buxton, ever alert to the attack, gave notice at once of a Motion on the subject and asked the Government their intentions. In his own words: 'they replied that they would undertake the question and "introduce a safe and satisfactory measure." I feel excessively relieved and delighted, and not a little thankful for this great mercy.' No government, indeed, could have ignored the powerful increase in public feeling. Christianity was everywhere marshalling its forces, shaking off its lethargy and preparing for victory. Mr. Stanley (later Lord Stanley), in introducing the Government Bill, said that the Anti-Slavery movement sprang from religious principle and thence came its strength.

Buxton's efforts were now concentrated on doing all in his power to ensure that the Government's promised Bill should be adequate and give early Emancipation. As one of his friends noted: 'He puts himself entirely out of the question. It does not seem to excite one feeling in his mind, whether, after all his toils, he is to appear in the matter or not. He seems to care for *nothing* but the advancement of the Cause.'

Just at the critical time when the Anti-Slavery leaders were most anxious to rouse public opinion, a young book-keeper named Whiteley arrived unexpectedly in England from the West Indies. He recounted to Buxton the everyday sufferings of the slaves as he himself had witnessed them. Buxton made him put down his experiences in writing. His account was printed as a pamphlet, and the printing presses of that day could not cope with the demand. Edition followed edition, until within a fortnight two hundred thousand copies had been sold. An important deputation to the Premier, led by Buxton and the two Gurneys, included 'merchants, squires, bankers, magistrates, clergymen and dissenting ministers from every part of the United Kingdom,' whilst petitions poured in from all parts of the country. On May 14 Stanley, as Colonial Secretary, introduced the Government Bill for the Abolition of Slavery throughout the British Dominions. Then Buxton and his colleagues knew that they had not laboured in vain, for Stanley used with great effect the very arguments and facts which they had made familiar to the House.

In a private conversation some years later Buxton said:

> I was amused to hear all my old arguments about population etc. which had so long been reviled and ridiculed, brought forward as if they were quite new, and applauded instead of laughed at. We were so delighted at carrying our measure, we were perfectly indifferent as to who did the deed.

But the Government proposals were far from being entirely satisfactory. Slavery was to be abolished and children under six were to be freed at once. But there was to be a twelve years' period of apprenticeship, during which the slaves were to work for their present masters. They were still to be liable to corporal punishment and the planters were to be compensated by a loan (afterwards changed into a gift) of £20,000,000. Buxton did not like the apprenticeship proposals, and he was vigorously censured by the more ardent of his followers for consenting to compensation.

But the only hope of success lay in accepting the Bill as a Government measure, and he was convinced that to attain their object (the statutory abolition of Slavery), concession and compromise were unavoidable. He refused to divide the House on the second reading, and voted for the grant to the planters. He moved, however, an amendment to limit apprenticeship to the shortest period necessary for establishing free labour, and suggested one year. This was lost, but only by seven votes, and Stanley agreed to reduce the period to seven years. (It was in fact terminated, as we shall see, after four years.)

On August 7, 1833, the Bill for the Total Abolition of Colonial Slavery passed the Lower House, and on August 20 it went through the House of Lords. The personal achievement of Buxton and his faithful handful had been astounding. Althorp said to Lushington: 'Well! you and Buxton have wielded a power too great for any individuals in this House. I hope we shall never see such another instance.' On another occasion, while Grey, the Prime Minister, was speaking to Buxton, Wellington remarked: 'If that individual is to have more power than Lords and Commons both, we may as well give up the Bill.' The comment of another member was: 'So after all the fanatics were right.'

Wilberforce died on July 29, but the passage of the Emancipation Bill was already assured, and he was able to 'Thank God that I should have lived to witness a day in which England is willing to give twenty million sterling for the Abolition of Slavery.' Buxton's decision, despite all the censure of his own extremists, not to oppose the second reading of the Bill, was warmly approved by the veteran leader, Clarkson, who wrote to Buxton: 'That the Bill is not entirely what I wished, I have no objection to confess; but yet I am thankful, inexpressibly thankful for it. I tremble to think what might have been the consequences, if you had refused the proposals of Parliament.' Buxton gave glory to God and in his characteristically practical way went straight ahead with schemes for the education and religious instruction of the negroes, whose Emancipation was to take effect on August 1, 1834.

There was great anxiety as to whether they would receive their freedom peacefully. Troops and war-ships were sent out to be at hand in case of disturbance.[1] Buxton, with the responsibility for Emancipation upon his shoulders, felt the anxiety intensely. His son and biographer records that

> he was at Northrepps Hall when on the 10th of September (1834) a large pile of letters came in with the Colonial stamps upon them. Well knowing that they would contain the long-looked for intelligence, he took them and walked out in the wood, desiring no witness but One, of the emotion and anxiety which he experienced. He opened them and deep indeed was his joy and gratitude to God, when he found that one letter after another was filled with accounts of the admirable conduct of the negroes on the great day of freedom. Throughout the Colonies the Churches and Chapels had been thrown open, and the slaves had crowded into them, on the evening of the 31st July. As the hour of midnight approached, they fell upon their knees and awaited the solemn moment, all hushed in silent prayer. When twelve sounded from the Chapel bells, they sprang upon their feet, and through every island rang the glad sound of thanksgiving to the Father of all, for the chains were broken and the slaves were free.[2]

[1] Lord Sligo, the Governor of Jamaica, reported in a letter to the Colonial Office in January, 1835, that no case of riot among the negroes had been reported ; the troops and ships had been recalled and ' it is impossible that matters can be better.'

[2] It is recorded that on the following Monday, three days later, they all returned quietly to work.

CHAPTER IV

The Aftermath of Slavery—Apprenticeship

Good Behaviour of Emancipated Negroes—Apprenticeship; its Drawbacks and Abuses—Houses of Correction—Joseph Sturge—His Visit to West Indies—Negro Progress—Building of Churches and Schools—Apprenticeship Abolished.

Lord Sligo, who became Governor of Jamaica in 1834, continued to send excellent reports of the good behaviour of the negroes, whilst the Bishop of Jamaica wrote, in 1835, that 'the industry of the negroes when working for wages has so entirely belied the apprehensions of the planters here that I have not a doubt of the entire success of the emancipation measure.'

But though legally emancipated on August 1, 1834, the negroes were, as we have seen, to be subject to apprenticeship for seven years and, before long, the news of their good behaviour began to be chequered by reports of their ill-treatment. Opinions differ greatly as to the condition of the negroes in general under apprenticeship. When Joseph Sturge visited the West Indies in 1837, he exposed some sensational cruelties and brought home with him a negro apprentice, James Williams, whom he had redeemed in order to rescue him from a long course of abominably cruel treatment. There is no doubt that the prisons and

Houses of Correction were dens of cruelty. But in many parts of the West Indies the apprentices were well treated, worked for far shorter hours than under slavery, and earned good enough wages to be able to save something. Dr. W. L. Mathieson, in his recent book 'British Emancipation,' has probably summed up the position accurately when he expresses the view that apprenticeship 'fell far short of Emancipation, but it certainly was not worse than Slavery.'

At the worst the apprenticed negro lived in the expectation of freedom at an early date, while under slavery he had nothing to live for and no hope of release save by death. Sligo, though he criticised its abuses severely, said that 'the want of complete success' was all that could be urged against it. The great majority of the planters disliked bitterly the Emancipation Act which had been forced upon them, and some, having no longer the 'property interest' which they had possessed when the negroes were their slaves, appeared to care even less than before whether they undermined the health of their apprentices by under-feeding or excessive punishments. They were abetted by the local legislatures, which revived oppressive laws which had become obsolete and devised new instruments such as vagrancy laws, laws to confine the negro to particular localities, wages acts, and laws to compel the apprenticeship of children. Lord Sligo and his equally humane and enlightened successor, Sir Lionel Smith, reported many abuses: 'Apprentices have had their food allowances stopped, often Saturdays taken from them. How then are they to exist without theft?'[1] In some cases they

[1] Sir Lionel Smith.

received only half the quantity of farinaceous food to which, even as slaves, they had been legally entitled. A forty-five hour week had been legally enacted, but was freely disregarded. The apprentices were punishable as vagabonds for going beyond bounds. One particularly objectionable practice was that of sentencing them to penal labour and then appropriating the labour to the use of their employers.

Although the flogging of women by overseers had been rendered illegal, they were still flogged by means of a legal quibble, under cover of prison discipline. Sir Lionel Smith, writing in 1837 to the Special Justices of Jamaica, commented on the severity of corporal punishments. In Mauritius, where the operation of the apprenticeship system was particularly oppressive, a quarter of the whole apprenticed population were punished in eleven months, 1835–36, more than half by flogging.

The Houses of Correction to which the apprentices, male and female, were committed, often for the most trivial offences, were described by Joseph Sturge as 'dens of pollution, outrage and cruelty.' The treadmill, recently introduced into West Indian prisons and of local manufacture, was nothing but an instrument of torture.

Mr. Lytton Bulwer,[1] the novelist, afterwards the first Lord Lytton, when speaking in the House of Commons in 1838 in support of the Bill for the immediate abolition of apprenticeship, referred to 'the Coroner's jury who, in the celebrated instance of the

[1] Lytton Bulwer was the first member of his family to be the champion of native races. The present holder of the title has continued the family tradition by his courageous work for the Abolition of Slavery.

woman tortured to death at the treadmill, returned a verdict of " Death by the visitation of God," ' and to ' Constables generally selected for their qualifications as slave-drivers.'

The local Justices of the Peace were drawn, as we have remarked in an earlier chapter, from the planting interests. But Special Magistrates were appointed to safeguard the interests of the negroes, and these men had indeed a difficult path before them. As Lord Glenelg remarked, when introducing in 1838 the Bill to amend the Abolition Act, ' Unless a Special Magistrate be a notorious partisan of the planter, nothing is too bad for him, whereas, for those who are called " Busha " Magistrates, that is, under the influence of the overseers, nothing is too good.' It is greatly to the credit of the majority of the Special Magistrates that Sligo could write of them : ' What was in the physical power of man to do, they did, and it is a matter of the greatest wonder and admiration that so much zeal, so much energy and such an indefatigable spirit of humanity as pervaded the vast majority should have been displayed by them."

The general sentiment of West Indian opinion appears to have been that to administer the apprenticeship in the spirit of the English Abolition Act was incompatible with the peace and prosperity of the Colonies. Antigua, which granted immediate and complete Emancipation in 1834 without any period of apprenticeship, was an honourable exception. The Jamaica Assembly remained true to its old tradition of resistance to every step taken for the amelioration and abolition of slavery. Sligo and his successor, Lionel Smith, were both attacked with the utmost violence.

Finally, the Home Government was forced to take the extreme step of suspending the Assembly.

It will be remembered that Buxton had accepted apprenticeship unwillingly for the time being, and moved an amendment to terminate it after one year. This was defeated, and he resigned himself to it. But Joseph Sturge and the more militant spirits in the Anti-Slavery movement were determined that it should be brought to a speedy end.

Joseph Sturge is a remarkable figure in the history of Emancipation. Born in 1793, the son of a Quaker farmer, near Bristol, he became a successful cornfactor in Birmingham. His twin interests were slavery and peace. He was a practical and vigorous Christian, who described himself as 'one of those who have never been able to see that a Christian was not equally bound to discharge his political with his religious duties.' 'When a Christian,' he said, 'is convinced that the principle on which he acts is correct, I believe it does not become him to examine too closely his probability of success.' He had none of the compromising instincts of a Parliamentarian, and had already, as we have seen, attacked Buxton for what he regarded as weak and sinful compromise in agreeing to compensation for the planters and apprenticeship for the slaves. He and his friends were not alone in their indignation with the planters for having perpetrated what they regarded as 'a practical and deliberate fraud' in accepting the £20,000,000 paid by the nation for the redemption of the slaves and then proceeding to turn apprenticeship into something which, in some of the islands at least, was almost indistinguishable from slavery.

Joseph Sturge and his friend Thomas Harvey determined to visit the West Indies to collect evidence. Cobden has left us an amusing picture of the visit paid by Sturge to Brougham which decided the former to take the voyage.

> Brougham [writes Cobden] told me of Sturge coming to him to arraign the conduct of the masters in the West Indies in oppressing their apprentices; how he (Brougham) laughed at him: 'Why, Joseph Sturge, how can you be such an old woman as to dream that you can revive the Anti-Slavery agitation to put an end to the apprenticeship?' How the quiet Quaker met him with this reply—'Lord Brougham, if when Lord Chancellor thou hadst a ward in Chancery who was apprenticed and his master was violating the terms of indenture, what would'st thou do?' How he felt this as a home thrust and replied 'Why, I should require good proof of the fact, Joseph Sturge, before I did anything.' How our friend rejoined—'Then I must supply thee with the proof.' How he packed his portmanteaux and quietly embarked for the West Indies, made a tour of the islands, collected the necessary evidence of the oppression that was being practised on the negro apprentices by their masters, the planters; how he returned to England and commenced an agitation throughout the country to abolish apprenticeship, to accomplish which it was necessary to reorganise all the old Anti-Slavery Societies which had been dissolved, or had laid down their arms . . . how he brought them again into the field and attained his object. [This is Cobden's description.]

The outcries of the planters at what they described as 'the lies of the infamous Sturge' may be imagined, but the actual outcome of his journey was that Parliament abolished apprenticeship as from August 1, 1838, three years before the date fixed by the Emancipation Act. Zachary Macaulay died in May, just too soon to hear the good news. Buxton had been severely criticised for doubting whether it was practicable to get apprenticeship shortened. Some time before Parliament abolished it (on the Motion of Sir Eardley Wilmot) he wrote to one of his old Anti-Slavery coadjutors: 'It seems just possible that the delegates may succeed, and if so, I am sure we shall both say "Thank God that other people had more courage and more discernment than ourselves."' By the time it was carried Buxton was no longer in Parliament (having been defeated at Weymouth in July, 1837). Nothing could have been warmer or more generous than his appreciation of Sturge, to whom he wrote:

> I bless God for the event; I bless God that He, who has always raised up agents such as the crisis required, sent you to the West Indies. I bless God that, during the Apprenticeship, not one act of violence against the person of a white man has, I believe, been perpetrated by a negro.

And in a letter to the Hon. Mrs. Upcher he said (May 23, 1838):

> I must write a line to tell you that Sturge and that party whom we thought all in the wrong are proved to be all in the right. A resolution for the immediate abolition of the Apprenticeship was carried by a majority of three last night. The intelligence was received with such a shout by the Quakers (myself among the number) that we strangers were all turned out for rioting! I am right pleased.[1]

This Motion was followed by a Bill introduced by Lord Brougham.

It is interesting to note that Disraeli voted for the termination of apprenticeship, while Gladstone, who

[1] Buxton was by this time no longer in Parliament, hence his presence in the Strangers' Gallery with the Friends.

had not yet emerged fully from the slave-owning traditions of his family, was in the opposite camp.

The despatch written by Lord Aberdeen, then Colonial Secretary, on the position of the negroes after the termination of apprenticeship is an admirable example of liberal principles. One extract must suffice:

> The great cardinal principle of the law for the abolition of Slavery [he wrote] is that the apprenticeship of the emancipated slaves is to be immediately succeeded by personal freedom, in that full and unlimited sense of the term in which it is used in reference to the other subjects of the British Crown. [He continued]: The preceding examination of colonial laws . . . will have exploded the idea of safety in leaving the welfare of the negroes to the care of colonial assemblies, or for the present to their own unaided exertions.

The Emancipators at home realised clearly that the negroes must be aided during their transition from slavery to freedom. The ink was hardly dry upon the Emancipation Act of 1833 before Buxton was at work on schemes for their education. After much expense and trouble he and Lushington were able to obtain a sum of over £110,000 left in 1710 by a certain Lady Mico 'for the redemption of white slaves in Barbary.' To this sum Government added a temporary grant of £20,000 a year to be used in educating the negroes. Both Buxton and Sturge gave generously of their own resources and the former took great trouble in interviewing personally the schoolmasters and missionaries who were sent out. Buxton maintained from the first that the training of native teachers was essential and gave them every encouragement. The negroes showed great zeal for education. The Baptist missionaries, formerly supported from this country, were now paid entirely by their own people, and well paid too. 'We learn from (the missionary) Knibb that from 1835 to 1840, in the three congregations under his care, no less than £11,000 had been raised for chapel building and education, and that in the whole Western Union the sum collected for these purposes amounted to £60,000. A sum of nearly £600 was subscribed to defray Knibb's expenses when he undertook a "legation" to the Anti-Slavery Society in 1840; and the flock of one of his colleagues, composed almost exclusively of black labourers, had raised as much as £2,600 in three and a half years. We read of a negro couple whose annual subscription to missions was £10, and of a widow whose "mite" for the chapel turned out to be five dollars.'[1]

The number of peasant proprietors increased rapidly. 'In little more than three and a half years after Emancipation, 3,315 negroes belonging to the Western Baptist Union had bought land and had spent on this purpose and on the building of their houses a total sum of £96,000.'[1]

Sir Charles Metcalfe, who succeeded Sir Lionel Smith as Governor of Jamaica in 1840, wrote thus:

> The thriving condition of the peasantry is very striking and gratifying . . . their behaviour is peaceable and in some respects admirable. They are fond of attending divine service and are to be seen on the Lord's day thronging to their respective churches and chapels, dressed in good clothes and many of them riding on horseback. They send their children to school and pay for their schooling. They subscribe for the erection of churches and chapels.

[1] W. L. Mathieson, *British Slave Emancipation*.

Would the negroes continue to work when they received their full freedom? That was the question which weighed upon the minds of the planters. In answering it, it must be remembered that where the negroes grew the bulk of their own food, as in Jamaica, they could be self-subsisting without working for wages, and that so long as they had only the simplest physical wants, wages offered but little inducement. The ordinary conditions of capital and labour were reversed and 'wage slavery' was impossible. Recently released slaves felt a very natural reaction against long hours of field work for their former masters. How were the latter to get their sugar canes weeded and harvested? The answer is that as slaves the negroes had not paid rent for their houses or for the grounds (usually virgin soil within the bounds of the estates) which they had cultivated and that rent was now the main instrument used, and often misused, by their former masters to make them work.

Another inducement, due to the survival of the traditional African attachment to land, was the strong desire to buy land for themselves. There was also a growing desire for new refinements and luxuries. Although there were, no doubt, some negroes so lazy as to justify Carlysle's cruel description of the 'Black Quashee,' many more were of the type described by Sir Charles Metcalfe, anxious to educate their children, to support their churches, to dress well and even to own horses and carriages. It was a blessing both for themselves and the planters that the religious instruction of the missionaries and their own peaceful dispositions had given them such a truly Christian spirit of peace and order that 'the whole slave population had passed at a bound from bondage to freedom without the slightest violation of order. . . . Not a single company of militia was maintained after emancipation, and seven years later it was stated in a magistrate's report that tranquillity had continued, though the police force consisted of 24 men and perhaps 250 rural constables, in nearly every instance estate labourers.' [1]

The abolition first of slavery, then of apprenticeship, gave a much-needed stimulus to the use of machinery. J. Davy, in 'The West Indies Before and Since Slave Emancipation,' 1854, remarks that a weeding machine with one horse, a man and a boy, had displaced 16 negroes in the weeding of canes. In British Guiana the compensation money was generally spent on improved machinery. A planter in St. Kitts said that before Emancipation everything was done by 'the thews and sinews' of the slaves. If lands were to be opened, instead of being ploughed, they were opened by means of the cane hoe; if a mountain was to be removed, it was all carried away upon the head piecemeal.' [2] In Antigua, in 1846, there were neither pitchforks nor wheelbarrows. As an institution for the encouragement of physical over-exertion in the slave and mental inertia in the owner, slavery is unequalled.

In spite of difficulties in obtaining labour, from which those employers who had ill-treated their apprentices naturally suffered most and the good employers comparatively little, the planters remained fairly prosperous until the British Government began to withdraw the protection for their products, amounting

[1] W. L. Mathieson, *British Slave Emancipation.*

[2] J. Davy, *The West Indies Before and Since Slave Emancipation,* 1854.

almost to a monopoly, which they had enjoyed in the home market. After several years of damaging uncertainty, the final blow was the Sugar Act of 1846, by which slave-grown sugar from foreign countries was admitted to Great Britain. Havana was illuminated, the sugar planters of Brazil and Cuba rejoiced, but to many planters in the West Indies it was an act of crushing severity, rendered still more severe by the fact that it coincided with the commercial crisis of 1847. The story of the unsuccessful opposition of the Anti-Slavery party in this country to the importation of slave-grown sugar is too long to be told here, and we must now see how the planters endeavoured to obtain the labour which they feared would be lost to them after the termination of slavery in 1833 and of apprenticeship in 1838.

CHAPTER V

The Aftermath of Slavery—Coolie Labour

First Indians Shipped—High Mortality—Flogging—French Colonies—The Recruiters—Fines—'Half Free'—'A Machine for sending Men to Prison'—'Protectors'—The India Office—Coolie Labour Abolished.

Africa being closed to them, the planters now looked to India. The origin of Indian Coolie labour, as it is commonly called, is described in the Report of the Committee set up in 1909 under the Chairmanship of Lord Sanderson, to enquire into 'Emigration from India to the Crown Colonies and Protectorates.' The Report states:

> In the early years of the 19th century certain sporadic attempts appear to have been made to engage labourers in Bengal to serve for a term of years in Mauritius and Réunion, but it was the abolition of slavery in the British Colonies in 1834 which gave the first great impetus to emigration.

On January 4, 1836, Mr. John Gladstone, Liverpool merchant, West Indian proprietor, and father of the rising young member for Newark, wrote as follows to a Calcutta firm with which his family were connected:

> We are in doubt . . . how far our negro apprentices in the West Indies may be induced to continue their services in the plantations after their apprenticeship expires in 1840.

We are therefore most desirous to obtain and introduce labourers from other quarters.

After giving a glowing account of the colony, the light labour, comfortable dwellings, abundance of good food, schools and religious instruction, he summed up by saying: 'It may fairly be said they pass their time agreeably and happily.' The Calcutta firm to whom he had addressed himself replied in encouraging terms that they had already sent several hundreds of men to the Mauritius, and added: 'We are not aware that any greater difficulty would present itself in sending men to the West Indies, the natives being perfectly ignorant of the place they go to or the length of voyage they are undertaking.'

Several large consignments of coolies were accordingly shipped, and John Gladstone obtained an Order in Council sanctioning labour contracts for five years, commencing on the arrival of the coolies in Demerara. This Order was issued on July 10, 1837, but it was not until January 3, 1838, that the public became aware of its existence, when it was denounced in the *British Emancipator*, an Anti-Slavery organ, as giving birth to a new slave trade.

The Calcutta Press stigmatised the so-called voluntary recruitment of the 'emigrants' as kidnapping. Private letters corroborated the fact that the coolies 'had to be forced on board,' that their treatment on the voyage was often extremely bad, and that the insanitary conditions resulted in a high mortality.

Scoble, Secretary of the Anti-Slavery Society, visited British Guiana, to which many of the coolies had been sent. He found a high death-rate, much sickness, bad housing conditions, insufficient food, much flogging, many runaways, and no legal provision for restoring the coolies to their own country. All of which was confirmed by a Government enquiry into John Gladstone's estate in that colony. Although he and other wealthy absentee proprietors regarded the complaints as the fabrications of agitators, there is no doubt that grave abuses existed, and after Buxton (in his last Parliamentary speech, July, 1837) had raised the question in the House of Commons and Brougham in the House of Lords, emigration was suspended by the Government and a Committee appointed in Calcutta to enquire into the whole matter.

In the words of Lord Sanderson's Report: 'Their report, which was submitted in 1840, showed clearly that abuses did undoubtedly exist with respect to recruitment in India.' Three of the members were altogether opposed to further emigration, but the fourth member, Sir J. P. Grant, recommended the reopening of emigration under certain safeguards. When the Committee's Report was presented to Parliament, in 1842, Grant's views won the day and emigration to Mauritius was resumed under safeguards. In 1844 it was permitted to Jamaica, British Guiana and Trinidad, in 1856 to Grenada, in 1858 to St. Lucia, and in 1860 to Natal. 'Between the years 1842 to 1870, operations were on a considerable scale. The total number of emigrants during these years was 533,595.'[1] Of these, 351,401 went to Mauritius, 79,691 to British Guiana, 42,519 to Trinidad, 15,169 to Jamaica, 7,021 to other West Indian Islands, 6,488 to Natal and 31,346 to French Colonies.

[1] Sanderson Report, Cd. 5192.

Lord Sanderson's Report states that 'methods of recruitment in India were gradually improved,' but much of the evidence received by the Committee proved the grave need for reform. Mr. J. A. Brown, an Indian civil servant of large experience, who appeared before the Committee at the request of the Indian Government, said :

> The recruiters are the worst kind of men they could possibly have. They are generally very low-class men, and as far as I understand, they are paid by the results, by the number of emigrants that they get. The consequence is that they very often try to entice married women away from their husbands.

It may be noted here that only 3 per cent. of the emigrants were women, and what that meant on the voyage and in the plantations may be imagined. Much evidence was given to show the deceptions practised upon the coolies to get them to sign an indenture.

The Sanderson Report states that 'when emigration was first opened to the West Indies, there was a very high death-rate both on the long sea journey and during the process of acclimatization.' 'A frightful mortality among the coolies' due to 'the neglect of proper sanitary precautions at a quarantine station in Mauritius' in 1856 is also described.

The Report remarks on the desire of the planters to retain their hold upon the coolies after the expiry of their period of indenture :

> The planters and the colonial governments, in which the planting interest is generally powerful, did not at first appreciate the fact that Indians make excellent settlers, and that it was to the advantage of the colony to encourage them to settle down as free citizens and so contribute to

the general prosperity. The aim of the planters, who had suffered so severely from the entire discontinuance of slave labour, was too often to acquire complete control over the labour market by means of regulations and administrative measures which aimed at compelling the coolie to re-enage himself on the expiry of his indenture, rather than encouraging free settlers.

Thus, in Natal,

Wages were paid only every two months and were subject to severe reductions in the shape of fines for absence. After the expiry of the indenture, immigrants were expected to reindenture. If they did not do so and worked for wages, they came under an ordinance applicable to native African labour, under which a servant was liable to whipping for neglect of work.

'Gross abuses' of a similar character were reported from British Guiana in 1870, and from Mauritius in 1867, and the Government of India appointed Commissions of Inquiry into these two colonies and Natal. One witness revealed frankly the desire nearest the heart of the planters: 'Anything which would tend to keep in the Colony able-bodied efficient labourers who are already acclimatised, in my opinion, would be good.' Accordingly, various devices were employed to extend the duration of the contracts for which the coolies had indentured themselves. For instance, the contracts for Fiji were for five years, but the labourer had to work for another five years before being allowed a 'free pass' back to India. In Jamaica a still more extraordinary contract was imposed. After the expiry of the initial indenture of five years, the coolie was known as a 'half free' for another term of five years. After completing ten years, he was allowed to embark for his home in India, provided that he paid one-third of the fare for his women relatives and half of his own. The same conditions prevailed in British Guiana, and after 1895 the screw was tightened upon the unfortunate coolies. While it is true that some attained to a position of some wealth in the Colonies, to the great majority this was impossible, and to ask them to pay sums quite beyond their powers for their return passages was, in fact, to compel them to exile for life. Recruitment should have been limited to five years, and full passage money granted at the end of that period.

The same attempt to use vagrancy laws as an instrument of constraint was made in respect of the Indian coolies, as we have already noticed in its application to the negro apprentices. Lord Sanderson's Report refers to 'the tendency, once again appearing in Mauritius, to treat Indian immigrants, when absent from their work, as vagrants, the Ordinance of 1889 being so framed as to allow of their arrest without warrant.'

The Report says of British Guiana: 'There is, however, one unsatisfactory feature of indentured immigration which is at least as prominent in this as in any of the other colonies, and that is the extent to which the employers resort to the criminal courts in order to enforce the fulfilment by the immigrants of their statutory obligations.' And, indeed, the returns for 1907–8 showed the extraordinary predilection of estate managers for the criminal courts. In British Guiana, with an indentured population of 9,784 persons, no less than 3,835 charges were preferred against the coolies under labour laws. In Trinidad, out of

11,506 coolies under indenture, 1,869 were convicted, and in Fiji, with 11,689 coolies, 2,291 were charged in the criminal courts.

The charges brought against the coolies were mainly under labour Ordinances for so-called 'malingering.' Mr. Edward Bateson, a magistrate of wide experience in the West and East Indies, informed the Committee :

> Sometimes people were brought before me either as vagrants or deserters, but the great majority of cases were idleness and alleged idleness, and it was impossible for me to ascertain really the merits of the case.

And again :

> complaints by masters or mistresses of insulting conduct, or words or gestures, and trumpery cases which ought not to have been brought into court, and which would not be brought in any other country before a criminal court.

To quote Bateson again : 'It is a very painful sight to see people being taken in batches to prison, handcuffed as if they were criminals, when they are not criminals in any sense.' The Government of India insisted that the Colonial Governments should appoint 'Protectors' for the coolies, but some of these protectors had an amazing conception of their duties. One of them, Commander W. H. Coombs of Trinidad, had estates of his own, and his point of view was solely that of the planters. He told the coolies that he would not 'stand any nonsense. You will either work for your pay on the estate, or you will work for Government for nothing in the gaol.' With such a 'Protector,' the position of indentured coolies in the courts was hopeless. Well might Sir George Robertson, a member of the Sanderson Committee, say to Bateson :

'It seems to me from what you have said that the coolie is absolutely defenceless,' to which Bateson replied: 'Absolutely,' and he added that he appeared to be placed in his position as stipendiary magistrate for the convenience of the employers: 'It resolved itself into that: I was a machine for sending men to prison.'

It is important to realise that the Government of India was at no time in favour of the immigration of coolie labourers and only agreed to it under pressure from *force majeure*, and even then only upon assurances of the acceptance of two principles of great importance concerning land and citizenship.

With regard to land, the Report states that

> the Government of India have constantly urged on the colonies the importance of making Crown lands easily available for the settlement of time-expired coolies. It is evident that the ultimate conversion of a large proportion of the indentured immigrants into an independent, prosperous and contented peasantry provides the best reply to a criticism of the system of indentured labour.

The principle regarding citizenship is expressed in Lord Salisbury's despatch of March 24, 1875:

> Above all things we must confidently expect, as an indispensable condition of the proposed arrangements, that the Colonial laws and their administration will be such that Indian settlers who have completed the terms of service to which they agreed, as the return for the expense of bringing them to the Colonies, *will be in all respects free men, with privileges no whit inferior to those of any other class of Her Majesty's subjects resident in the Colonies.*[1]

Not all the support of public opinion was able to get these two principles invariably applied, but the con-

[1] Italics mine.—J. H.

stant pressure that was maintained for the improvement of the system, and finally the Great War, put a stop to Indian immigration into all British Colonies as from January 1, 1920, and thus ended a not very creditable or satisfactory chapter in our colonial history.

It is true that the indentured labour system enabled a good many coolies to earn more than in their own country and to become successful colonists, but it was capable of degenerating into something closely akin to slavery. The intention of its originators was simply to substitute cheap Indian labour for slave labour, and in spite of the watchfulness of the Government of India, it afforded only too much scope for the exploitation and often oppressive treatment of ignorant and helpless people far removed from their own country, and it is no wonder that it has often aroused justifiable resentment amongst their fellow countrymen in India.

The Government of India deserves credit for its frequent protests, but the planters, like the Bourbons, had learnt nothing and forgotten nothing and they opposed reforms suggested by the Indian Government with the same tenacity that their predecessors had displayed in opposing the reforms and ameliorations of slavery suggested by the Colonial Office. As with slavery, so with indentured labour, the only solution for its evils was abolition. But it took many years to secure this. Buxton began the struggle in 1837, but it took his successors in the Anti-Slavery and Aborigines' Protection Society nearly eighty years to reform it out of existence. Aided by the political consequences of the Great War, its abolition was at last achieved.

CHAPTER VI

The Aftermath of Slavery—Aborigines' Protection

The Aborigines Committee—A Great Charter—Buxton's 'Three Great Objects'—The Kaffir War of 1835—Land—Nine Principles of Government.

In his own day Buxton's work for the protection of native races attracted less attention than the outstanding achievement of Emancipation, but to us to-day it is in some respects, perhaps, of even greater value, for whilst opportunities for the legal enslavement of native races by Europeans are now, thank God, rare, temptations to exploitation are as great as in Buxton's day, and it is to his vision, insight and practical understanding that we owe principles upon which we are still working in our advance towards the ideal of Trusteeship. Exhausted though he was in health, he did not rest upon his laurels after carrying the Emancipation Bill through Parliament in 1833, for in the following year we find him writing to his friend, Dr. Philip, of the London Missionary Society in Cape Town: 'I stay in Parliament very much against my inclination, for no other purpose except to watch the West Indies and to protect the aborigines, chiefly the latter.'

In 1835 he determined to devote the remainder of his

life to 'three great objects now on my hands. 1st, the completion of emancipation, for much requires to be done. 2nd, the abolition of the Spanish and Portuguese Slave Trade. 3rd, the just treatment of the aborigines.'

The Kaffir War of 1835, in which 4,000 Kaffirs were killed, 60,000 herd of their cattle captured, and their territory of Adelaide taken from them, increased his ardour, and he succeeded in obtaining the appointment of a Parliamentary Committee to enquire into the war, as well as into the general treatment of the aboriginal nations bordering on our settlements.

As a result of the Committee's enquiry, Lord Glenelg, then Colonial Secretary, decided that the Adelaide territory had been unjustly taken from the Kaffirs. 'Lord Glenelg,' wrote Buxton to Zachary Macaulay,

> has sent a most noble despatch to the Cape of Good Hope, restoring the territory we lately stole to the Kaffirs, and laying down the soundest principles with respect to future intercourse with them.

Amongst other practical reforms, the Government agreed to appoint Protectors of the Aborigines in every colony where the English came in contact with them.

Buxton had long realised the fundamental importance of the land question, and he had already written to Dr. Philip :

> It appears to me that we ought to fix and enforce certain regulations and laws with regard to the natives of all countries where we make settlements. These laws must be based on the principles of justice. In order to do justice, we must admit, first, that the natives have a right to their own lands.

The Parliamentary Committee entrusted Buxton

who was its Chairman, with the writing of its Report, and, regarding the Aborigines question as of the very greatest importance in the future, he endeavoured to make the Report a manual for their future treatment. He has thus left us a practical heritage in principles and suggestions of permanent value, and it is right and fitting that his last Parliamentary action should have been the presentation of the Aborigines Report.

Writing to his brother-in-law, J. J. Gurney, he describes the Report as

> a fair compendium of the evidence given before the Committee during three years . . . and I have little doubt it will go far to check that desperate and wide spreading villainy which has rendered the intercourse of the civilised and Christian man with the savage little else than one uniform system of cruelty, rapacity and murder.

The Committee, which included Gladstone, Lushington and Sir George Grey, was 'appointed to consider what measures ought to be adopted with regard to the native inhabitants of countries where British settlements are made, and to the neighbouring tribes, in order to secure to them due observance of justice, and the protection of their rights, to promote the spread of civilization among them, and to lead them to the peaceful and voluntary reception of the Christian religion.'

The Committee's Report is well worth careful study to-day. It begins by describing in some detail what was often disgraceful treatment of natives by Europeans in Newfoundland, North and South America, New Holland (Australia), Van Diemen's Land, the Pacific Islands and South Africa. It is a melancholy story (to quote its own words) of 'the desolating effects of the association of unprincipled Europeans with natives in a ruder state.'

The Report continues :

> It is not too much to say, that the intercourse of Europeans in general, without any exception in favour of the subjects of Great Britain, has been, unless when attended by missionary exertions, a source of many calamities to uncivilised nations. As a nation we have not hesitated to invade many of the rights which they hold most dear.

The Report emphasises, on the other hand,

> the effect of fair dealing and of Christian instruction upon heathens. These instances are unhappily less numerous than those of an opposite character, but they are not less conclusive.

Much evidence is produced showing the value of the educative, civilising and peacemaking labours of the missionaries.

The principal recommendations made by the Committee were a veritable Charter of Native Rights :

> I. *Protection of natives to devolve upon the Executive.* . . . This is not a trust which could conveniently be confided to the local legislatures. . . . The settlers in almost every colony, having either disputes to adjust with the native tribes, or claims to urge against them, the representative body is virtually a party, and therefore ought not to be the judge in such controversies. . . . The Governor of each colony should be invested by Her Majesty . . . with authority for the decision of all questions affecting the interests of the native tribes.
>
> II. *Contracts for Service to be limited.* No vagrancy laws or other regulations should be allowed, the effect of which might be to cripple the energies of the natives by preventing them selling their labour at the best price, and at the market most convenient to themselves. All contracts . . . should

be expressly limited in their duration to a period which should, in no case, exceed 12 months. . . . Every contract for service should be made in the presence of an officer specially appointed for that purpose, in whom should be vested a summary jurisdiction to enforce the payment of the stipulated wages. To the neglect of regulations of this kind is to be ascribed the growth of a servile relation, differing little from slavery.

III. Sale of ardent spirits to be prevented.

IV dealt with the vital question of native lands:

So far as the lands of the Aborigines are within any territories over which the dominion of the Crown extends, the acquisition of them by Her Majesty's subjects, upon any title of purchase, grant, or otherwise, from their present proprietors, should be declared illegal and void.

Alas, how many injustices would have been prevented and how different would have been the development of huge areas of the world if our legislators of the last hundred years had adhered to these sound principles!

V recommended that new territories are not to be acquired without the sanction of the Home Government.

VI recommended that 'Religious instructions and education be provided' to be charged to the revenue of each colony, and points out that 'the ancient lords of the wilderness have been dispossessed,' that the land has since been sold by Europeans for high prices, and concludes by saying that

it requires no argument to show that we thus owe to the natives a debt, which will be but imperfectly paid by charging the land revenue of each of those provinces with whatever expenditure is necessary for the instruction of the adults, the education of their youth, and the protection of them all.

VII is also in line with the best modern methods

of colonial administration. It deals with the punishment of crimes and the hardship of making

> ignorant savages . . . amenable to a code of which they are absolutely ignorant, and the whole spirit and principles of which are foreign to their modes of thought and action. . . . It would, therefore, on every account, be desirable to induce the tribes in our vicinity to concur in devising some simple and effectual method of bringing to justice such of their own people as might be guilty of offences against the Queen's subjects. For that purpose, treaties might be made with the chiefs of the independent tribes, defining, with all practicable simplicity, what acts should be considered as penal, by what penalties they should be visited, and in what form of procedure those penalties should be enforced.

VIII recommends that

> as a general rule . . . it is inexpedient that treaties should be frequently entered into between the local Governments and the tribes in their vicinity. Compacts between parties negotiating on terms of such entire disparity are rather the preparatives and the apology for disputes than securities for peace: as often as the resentment or the cupidity of the more powerful body may be excited, a ready pretext for complaint will be found in the ambiguity of the language in which their agreements must be drawn up, and in the superior sagacity which the European will exercise in framing, in interpreting and in evading them.

IX urges that missionaries, 'those gratuitous and invaluable agents,' should be protected and assisted, but concludes with a judicious word of advice to the missionary:

> It is necessary that, with plans of moral and religious improvement, should be combined well-matured schemes for advancing the social and political improvement of the tribes, and for the prevention of any sudden changes which might

be injurious to the health and physical constitution of the new converts.

The Report as a whole shows a far-sighted and practical grasp of the principles and, to a great extent, the practice by which the most enlightened colonial administrators of the present day are guided. These principles have from the start inspired the Aborigines Protection Society, which was founded in 1837, with Buxton as its President, 'to assist in protecting the defenceless and promoting the advancement of uncivilised tribes,' and which, from that day to this, has worked for these ends. The Aborigines Protection Society and the British and Foreign Anti-Slavery Society, though to some extent composed of the same persons, existed as separate bodies until the year 1909. They frequently co-operated, but sometimes adopted different lines of policy. It was to prevent overlapping and to make for more efficient working that both Societies joined forces in 1909.

CHAPTER VII

The Aftermath of Slavery—Buxton's Last Years

Foreign Slave Trade—Prince Albert and the Niger Expedition—Its 'Failure'—Buxton's Ill-health—Death—His Tomb in Westminster Abbey.

No book written upon the hundred years' work of Emancipation would be complete without reference to the attempt to combat the evil of slavery from a new angle which occupied and saddened the last years of Buxton's life. His attempt is thus described in the inscription on his tomb in Westminster Abbey: 'The energies of his mind were afterwards concentrated on a great attempt to extinguish the Slave Trade in Africa, by the substitution of agriculture and commerce and by the civilising influence of the Gospel.'

The apparently insuperable difficulties of abolishing the foreign and African Slave Trade had long weighed on his mind. In 1835 he had moved an Address for making our treaties on this subject with foreign powers more stringent and the penalties of the crime more severe. The idea that struck him forcibly in 1837 was this, that 'though strong external measures ought still to be resorted to, the deliverance of Africa was to be effected by calling out her own resources.' Lord Palmerston, Buxton wrote, had been led 'to the same conclusion as my own, viz. that the Slave Trade is to be abolished by legitimate trade.'

Accordingly, he made laborious investigations into the trade and commercial resources of West Africa, and after collecting much evidence and interviewing nearly all the Ministers, he wrote a letter to Lord Melbourne embodying his ideas. The scheme which he proposed included an expedition up the Niger to develop trade and peaceful relations with the inhabitants, a trading company promoted by private individuals, a model agricultural farm, and the sending of missionaries. He urged the importance of making use of native agency, especially in view of the deadly climate. Buxton's plan was warmly received by Ministers, for the Cabinet appears to have considered the potential advantage to England, as well as to Africa, from opening a vast new field to commerce, of such importance as to justify the Government in attempting to carry the plan into effect. Buxton notes, however, that 'our friend, Joseph Sturge, who is somewhat restive about my Slave Trade views, won't go along with us.'

But with such powerful support from the Government the scheme was launched. Prince Albert gave it his support by presiding at a great public meeting of the African Civilisation Society held in Exeter Hall on June 1, 1840. Three steamers, the *Albert*, the *Wilberforce* and the *Soudan*, were fitted out by the Government and inspected by the Prince Consort before they sailed in the spring of 1841.

Buxton wrote to tell Sir John Jeremie, now Governor of West Africa, of his hopes for the expedition and of the day of prayer for its success which he had arranged should take place in all the churches in the country. He attended no less thoroughly to every detail in the outfitting of the ships that might serve to protect the crews from the dreaded climate.

Every human precaution was taken, but in vain. The expedition started well, and Commander Bird Allen, who commanded one of the ships, has left an interesting description of the friendliness of the natives, the busy market place at Goree (a town several hundred miles up the Niger) crowded with people and with goods which read like a list of the gifts brought by the Queen of Sheba to King Solomon: 'Country cloths, camwood in balls, ironwork, twine, silk, straw hats with enormous brims, platters of wood and calabashes beautifully carved.' Bird Allen described the joy of some slaves whom he had persuaded their owners to liberate.

But before long almost all the Englishmen were attacked by 'malignant fever' and two of the ships were forced to return to sea. The heroic Bird Allen still pushed forward on the *Albert.* Then he too was stricken, his ship forced to turn back, and he died at Fernando Po. Of the 301 persons who composed the expedition when it commenced the ascent of the Niger, 41 perished of fever, but it is worth noting that of the 150 Africans on board, not one died of the disease. Of the Englishmen a contemporary writer remarks: 'To its officers and men, dead as well as living, the highest credit appears to be due. They conquered everything but impossibilities: nature they could not conquer.'

The failure of the Niger expedition almost broke Buxton's heart, and although he lived for three years more, it was the final blow to his broken health. His biographer writes:

> His health became gradually more feeble and he could no longer bear any sustained mental exertion. He was only 55 years of age; but already the evening was come of his day of ceaseless toil, nor was its close brightened by the beams of success and joy. The idea of what he so forcibly called 'the incomparable horrors' of the slave-trade had fastened itself on his mind with the most vivid reality; the burning and plundered villages of Africa, the ships traversing the Atlantic with their cargoes of torture—these pictures were ever before him. When unconscious that he was observed, he would at times utter such groans as if his heart was sinking beneath its load. He rarely spoke of the Expedition, scarcely alluded to Captain Bird Allen's death, but his grave demeanour, his worn pale face, the abstraction of his manner and the intense fervour of his supplication that God would 'pity poor Africa,' these showed too well the poignancy of his feelings.[1]

His cherished scheme for the constructive regeneration of Africa had failed, but we who see to-day the development of West Africa in prosperity and civilisation shall not feel that his attempt was altogether in vain, still less shall we feel that his principle, 'the deliverance of Africa by the calling out of her own resources,' was at fault. Lord John Russell, speaking at the melancholy meeting of the African Civilisation Society which took place after the failure of the expedition, came forward with his usual courage and asserted boldly that it had been based on sound principles. History has in fact demonstrated to the hilt that Buxton's principles were sound. From his

[1] *Memoirs of Sir T. Fowell Buxton*, by C. Buxton.

beloved friend, Bishop Middleton of Calcutta, came letters of comfort and hope: 'Be not cast down, my dearest friend, nothing we do for God in the cause of humanity is lost.'

During this time of ill-health and disappointment his love of nature remained a consolation, and his plantations of young trees at Northrepps were a great interest to him. One of his friends remarked to him that his plantations would 'some day be the pride of the country, if England stands.' 'England stand,' said he, with a touch of his old fire. 'I will never believe that any country will fail, which has abolished Slavery as England has done.'

In 1843 came an alarming increase of bodily and mental weakness, but in January, 1844, he rallied for a time and addressed a clear and vigorous letter to Sir Robert Peel, then Prime Minister, on the grave danger of encouraging slavery and the slave trade by the proposal to admit slave-grown sugar from Cuba and Brazil into this country. Peel's reassuring reply included a warm tribute to 'the untiring friend of humanity and of the African race.'

A few months before his death he wrote a long letter to Lord Stanley, then Colonial Secretary, urging him to abandon a proposed scheme for obliging liberated Africans at Sierra Leone to emigrate to the West Indies. He feared anything approximating to compulsory emigration and objected strongly to breaking up in any degree the system of training and education at Sierra Leone which was just beginning to produce results of importance to the whole Continent of Africa. In his state of extreme weakness, the composition of the letter cost him an almost superhuman effort. His son writes that he would ' sink back exhausted in the middle of a sentence, then rouse himself, and try again, till at last it was completed. . . . But it scarcely displays any trace of the extreme debility under which he was labouring. With this act closed his long and arduous exertions on behalf of the negro race.'

Ten days before his death he began talking, apparently in his sleep, of the conversion of the heathen and of longing to be at work for them. 'I am ready to undertake all the working part,' he said. These last words are characteristic of the man.

He died on February 9, 1845. The inscription on his tomb in Westminster Abbey gives a true picture of a great Christian, a great reformer and a tireless worker in the cause of suffering humanity.

Endued with a vigorous and capacious mind,
of dauntless courage and untiring energy,
He was early led by the love of God,
To devote his powers to the Good of Man.

In Parliament, he laboured
For the improvement of prison discipline,
For the amendment of the Criminal Code,
For the suppression of suttees in India,
For the Liberation of the Hottentots in Southern Africa,
And, above all
For the emancipation of eight hundred thousand slaves
in the British Dominions.
In this last righteous enterprise,
After ten years of arduous conflict,
A final victory was given
to him and his co-adjutors,
' By the good Hand of our God '
On the memorable 1st of August 1834.

The energies of his mind were afterwards concentrated
On a great attempt
to extinguish the slave trade in Africa,
By the substitution of agriculture and commerce,
And by the civilizing influence of the Gospel.

Exhausted in mind and body
'He fell asleep'
Reposing in faith on his Redeemer,
in the 59th year of his age.

This Monument is erected
By his friends and fellow-labourers
at home and abroad;
Assisted by the grateful contributions
of many thousands of the African race.

CHAPTER VIII

Victorian Struggles

Labour in South Africa—Land Struggles—Foreign Slave Trade—Spanish Trade—World Slavery Conference—French Slavery — French Emancipators — Brazilian Slavery—Turkish Slavery—General Gordon and the Soudan—Slavery in Morocco—Situation in Indian States —Zanzibar Slavery.

When Queen Victoria came to the throne, the attitude of the English people towards slavery had undergone a deep and lasting change, thanks to Wilberforce, Buxton and their helpers. Since their day few Englishmen have ever attempted to defend slavery.

The Victorian age was one of steady pressure by the Anti-Slavery forces, but not one during which public opinion in this country was again stirred as profoundly and widely as by the great step taken in 1833. Never again would slavery be tolerated for long in British possessions, *provided that it was recognised as slavery.*

But although the Anti-Slavery Society and the Aborigines Protection Society (the colleagues and descendants of the great Emancipators) were quick to recognise slavery in its new disguises, it was more difficult for the general public to be stirred by a series of skirmishes than by one great engagement.

In the British Empire the period covers great progress in spite of grave abuses such as Kanaka Labour and Indian Coolie Labour, 'regrettable incidents' like the Borneo massacre, occasional massacres of the aborigines in Australia and Indians in North America, atrocious incidents of commercial exploitation, and the still more serious and increasing aggressions of commercial imperialism in South Africa, where the land hunger of the English and Dutch settlers led to almost complete disregard of the rights of the unfortunate natives over their own soil. These abuses and aggressions have left behind them grave evils, and they must always weigh heavily upon our national conscience. But they do not lessen the inestimable moral and practical value of the example given to the world by the Emancipation Act of 1833.

So deep was the impression made by that event that for a short time public opinion in this country seems to have been under the illusion that the fight was won for good and all, and that the Emancipators could now sing their *Nunc Dimittis*. The Anti-Slavery Society was even dissolved after the Emancipation Act became law.[1] But it was very soon realised that as Sir Robert Peel put it in 1840, our people had done 'no more than rescue their own character from the degradation in which the slave trade (and slavery) had involved them.' The British Anti-Slavery Society was reconstituted in 1839 as 'The British and Foreign Anti-Slavery Society,' and worked in close touch with the Aborigines Protection Society, founded by Buxton in 1837 'to assist in protecting the defenceless and promoting the advancement of uncivilised tribes,' until

[1] W. L. Mathieson, *British Slave Emancipation*.

the two were united in 1909. Their work was so closely allied for many years that it will generally be convenient to describe them as one throughout this chapter. The tasks before the Anti-Slavery Society were to abolish the very considerable remnants of slavery in the British Empire, to continue the uphill task of abolishing foreign slave-trading and slave-owning, and to aid the American Abolitionists in their mighty endeavour. Next, and this part of the work is still in its early stages, to abolish slavery in those countries of Asia and Africa in which it then flourished and still persists.

Both Societies were keenly alive to the emergence of new forms of disguised slavery (the many forms of Contract Labour, Indentured Labour, debt bondage, etc.) which appeared in one country after another as slavery ceased to be either reputable or legal. The never-ending attempts to reintroduce slavery by calling it a new name reminds one of nothing so much as of the struggle of Hercules with the monster which took on a new shape each time that he believed himself to have dealt it the final blow. Slaves became 'Apprentices,' 'Contract Labourers,' 'Emancipados,' 'Emigrés Libres,' 'Serviçaes.' Negro slavery being discountenanced, Indian Indentured labourers, South Sea Islanders and Chinese Coolies were obtained in their place.

The work of the Aborigines Protection Society, founded by Buxton, with unfailing instinct for the needs of the future, has continued to grow in importance to the present day.

If that part of its work which, during the first half

of Queen Victoria's reign, dealt with the protection of the Red Indians and Australian aborigines is less prominent to-day, it is largely because these ill-used races have, alas, so decreased in numbers as no longer to excite fear in the white populations. But it is also because, thanks to the advocacy and example of those who went before us, our standards of humanity are now so much higher that the grosser outrages of the past could hardly take place to-day.

The main aspects of the work of the reformers—the education and political emancipation of the formerly subject races, the supreme necessity of giving them their fair share of their own land, the many burning questions connected with labour and taxation—all these continue to concern us as closely as they concerned our Victorian predecessors. Buxton and those who succeeded him in the work of the two Societies understood almost all the problems that confront us to-day. The records of the two Societies show that they apprehended as clearly as we do the great complex of South African problems; the white man's fear of being swamped by the native races, the greed which caused the whites to grasp more and more of the land and its inevitable conflict with the passionate attachment of the natives to their own land. The land problem is as acute as ever. On the other hand, there is probably less physical cruelty inflicted by white men upon native races to-day, and in that direction our task should be easier than that of our forerunners.

Queen Victoria's reign was an age of colonial expansion during which all the great Powers staked their conflicting claims for larger and larger shares of African soil. They acquired territory in various ways, sometimes through the aggressions of the great commercial companies, such as the British South Africa Company, sometimes by treaty extension of their spheres of influence. The Congo Free State was such a unique instance of commercial exploitation that it deserves a separate chapter.

Foreign countries continued to carry on the Slave Trade despite treaty engagements and pledges. Many protests were addressed by the Anti-Slavery Society in this country to crowned heads and governments. Deputations visited the capitals of Europe and enthusiasts from this country did their best to found anti-slavery societies in other countries. A few noble spirits responded: Señor Vizcarrondo, the founder of the Spanish Anti-Slavery Society, who suffered imprisonment for his opinions; Señor Nabuco, a tower of strength in Brazil for many years; Dr. Schweinfurth of Germany; and a few distinguished Frenchmen who included M. de Tocqueville, M. Schoelcher, and most ardent and famous of all, Cardinal Lavigerie, Archbishop of Algiers.

American Emancipation is the outstanding event of this period, and Abraham Lincoln towers above every other figure, but it is impossible in the space of this small volume to depict the great struggle for American Emancipation, which would require a volume to itself, or even to name its many heroes.

The foreign Slave Trade, and in particular that carried on by Spain, Portugal, Brazil and France, called first for the efforts of the Anti-Slavery leaders.

In 1836 the British Commissioners in Sierra Leone reported that:

'There is nothing in the experience of the past year to show that the Slave Trade of Portugal or Spain has in any degree diminished.'

Although Talleyrand had announced to Lord Castlereagh on July 30, 1815, 'that on the part of France the traffic in slaves should cease, from the present time, everywhere and for ever,' the trade was still carried on, and to an enormous extent, by French subjects under the protection of the French flag.

Very large numbers of African slaves were imported into Brazil—114,288 into five ports alone—in the year and a half ending June 30, 1830. The horrors and mortality attendant on the Slave Trade remained unabated. A few cases will suffice.

In February, 1835, a 200-ton Spanish brig, the *Formidable*, left Africa for Brazil with 712 slaves on board: 304 died on the voyage. On another Spanish bark, the *Minerva*, bound from Calabar to Sierra Leone, 200 died out of 725; and on another Spanish schooner, the *Sutil*, 106 died out of 325. The slaves were so tightly packed that according to an eye-witness in Sierra Leone: 'Once so fixed, relief by motion or change of posture is unattainable. The body frequently stiffens into a permanent curve, and in the streets of Freetown, I have seen liberated slaves in every conceivable state of distortion. . . . Many can never resume the upright posture.'

When Sir Robert Peel addressed the African Civilisation Society at Exeter Hall (in the presence of the Prince Consort) on June 1, 1840, he said: 'I want to impress upon your minds that in granting the twenty millions [paid in compensation to the West Indian planters] the people of England did no more than to rescue their own character from the degradation in which the Slave Trade had involved them . . . the Trade is yet in all its sinful vigour.' He went on to describe 'the recent wreck of two slavers off Mazalangie Harbour. The crew and 200 slaves were saved. It was reported that those vessels had 900 slaves on board; but during a hurricane the hatches were battened down, and, on opening them, 300 slaves were found to have died of suffocation. Again the hurricane came on, the hatches were again battened down and 300 more were suffocated from the same cause; and 100 died upon the passage. What was the course pursued by the crews under such awful circumstances? They returned to Mazalangie for the purpose of getting a fresh supply of unhappy slaves.'

Such were the horrors of the Slave Trade thirty-three years after British Abolition. The enormous extent to which *slave-owning* existed is shown by the fact that under Christian Governments alone the slave population in 1841 is estimated to have numbered 6,397,300. If the slaves in the not professedly Christian countries in which slavery survives to-day had been added the numbers would probably have been doubled.[1]

An International Conference was obviously required to deal with what were mainly world problems, and accordingly, in June, 1840, the first Anti-Slavery

[1] It is estimated that there are to-day between 5,000,000 and 6,000,000 enslaved persons in the world. Abolitionists can be encouraged by feeling that 100 years of effort has at least reduced the evil to half its proportions.

World Convention assembled at the Freemasons' Tavern in London. The famous painter and more famous diarist, Haydon, has immortalised the scene in the picture which hangs to-day in the National Portrait Gallery. The spirits of Wilberforce, Sharp and the heroic Toussaint l'Ouverture are symbolically represented. The veteran pioneer, Thomas Clarkson, is shown, surrounded by all the leading Abolitionists of the day, with M.P.'s, Quakers and supporters from every part of the country. From France and the U.S.A. came distinguished delegations, the latter including the celebrated Lucretia Mott and other women delegates[1] from the Massachusetts and Pennsylvania Societies. The American Quaker poet, Whittier, sent a stirring ode. The proceedings opened with prayer. Haydon, a man of the world, not easily moved by what he called 'benevolent meetings,' has thus described the moment when the whole assembly answered the prayer of the aged Clarkson with their twice-repeated 'Amen.'

> That deep toned Amen [he writes] came on my mind like the knell of a departing curse. I looked about me on the simple and extraordinary people, ever ready with their purse and their person for the accomplishment of their great object ; and if ever sound was as an echo to the sense, or if ever deep and undaunted meaning was conveyed to the depths of the soul, the death warrant of slavery all over the world was boded by that Amen !

[1] The women delegates were exiled to the Gallery after the opening session, owing to the prevailing prejudice against the participation of their sex on public Committees with men. The three hours' debate which decided their exclusion seems to have been the only inharmonious note struck during the Conference.

A second World Convention was held in London in 1843 and both were vigorously followed up by the Anti-Slavery Society. Addresses on Slavery and the Slave Trade were presented to the crowned heads and governments of a great part of the world.[1]

Deputations were sent to Spain and Portugal and an interview was obtained with the King of France. Joseph Sturge, who had played a most active part in organising the World Convention, visited the U.S.A. to promote co-operation between the British and American Anti-Slavery Societies and to remove the objections of the American 'Friends' to taking part in Anti-Slavery propaganda. He had thoughts of visiting Brazil and Cuba, but his influence with the Quakers decided him to go to the U.S.A. instead. There is no doubt that his encouragement was of real value to the hardly pressed American Abolitionists, of whom William Lloyd Garrison, the poet Whittier and the great Unitarian Minister, William Ellery Channing, were at that time amongst the most notable.

The full story of the long-drawn struggle against foreign slave-trading and slave-owning would fill many volumes. It must be remembered that the Anti-Slavery leaders had no League of Nations to help them, and that the international treaties (described in a later chapter), though invaluable as a prelude to greater things, were to a large extent ineffectual owing to the lack of permanent international machinery for

[1] These included Great Britain, the President of the U.S.A., Austria, Bavaria, Denmark, Greece, France, Holland, Portugal, Prussia, Russia, Spain, Saxony, Sardinia, Switzerland, the Argentine, Brazil, Mexico, the Ottoman Empire, the Canton of Zurich and the Free City of Frankfort.

carrying them out. A cynic, indeed, would probably divide most of the countries concerned into two classes—not sheep and goats, but two kinds of goats—those which openly obstructed all reform and those which promised but did not perform. Over and over again, in one country or another, slave-trading and slave-owning were abolished but only on paper, and the long tale of evasions and delays would have exhausted the energy of the reformers and destroyed all their faith in human nature, had not deceptions and delays been balanced by victories of humanity and justice.

The limitations of space will only permit the barest outline of the progress and struggles of the Victorian era in foreign countries.

As pointed out in the previous chapter, France had declared slave-trading illegal in 1815. But owing to the persistent refusal of her Government to permit the right of search, the trade was continued on a large scale under the French flag. In 1888 the abuse of the French flag by Arab slave dhows was exposed by the French Anti-Slavery Society, and by Mr. Sydney Buxton in the House of Commons. It was proved that in Madagascar, Zanzibar, Pemba and the South Indian Ocean generally the surreptitious use of the French flag to cover the Slave Trade was very extensive. In 1893 the Annual Report of the British and Foreign Anti-Slavery Society noted that 'owing to the refusal of the French Government to permit the right of search which had been agreed to by almost every other nation . . . cases were constantly coming under the notice of the Society of slave traffic carried on in the Red Sea and the Indian Ocean under the French Flag.'

The great step of abolishing slave-owning in all her possessions was taken by France in 1848, and for this action great credit is due to the French Abolitionists—aided by their colleagues in this country. (The British Society sent deputations to Paris in 1840, 1842 and 1844.) But even after the abolition of slave-owning great watchfulness continued to be required, for in 1852 the French Government began the practice of introducing African negroes into their colonies under the euphemistic title of 'emigrés libres.' In 1857, 1858 and 1859 this question was discussed in the British Parliament, and the French Emperor ordered enquiries to be made. In 1863 the attention of the British Government was called to 'the sale by the Pasha of Egypt to the French of 450 Nubians for service in Mexico.'

The story of French efforts to substitute Indian coolie labourers for negro slaves is very similar to our own. For a good many years the Government of India permitted the recruiting of Indian coolies for the French Colonies of St. Pierre, Réunion, Martinique, Guadaloupe and Cayenne. M. Victor Schoelcher, Deputy for Martinique and later Senator, whose exertions on behalf of the coloured races in the French Colonies earned for him the title of 'the Wilberforce of France,' made many protests against the ill-treatment of the Indian coolies. They were overworked, underfed, their death-rate was excessive, and the planters used them, to quote the words of a French Government Commission of which M. Schoelcher was a member, 'as being merely instruments of agriculture.' M. Schoelcher attended a meeting of the Anti-Slavery Society in London in 1878 and stated that the treatment of

Indian coolies in the French Colonies demanded the urgent attention of the English people. Finally the permission to import Indian coolies into French Colonies was cancelled by the Government of India.

Madagascar, which had long been under French influence and had had a French Resident since 1885, was formally recognised by Great Britain as a French Protectorate in 1890, and the French Government became responsible for putting an end to the slave-trading and slavery which still persisted, although in 1875 the Christian Queen of Madagascar had granted freedom to the Mozambique slaves. In 1877 slave-trading from Madagascar had been nominally abolished, but ten years later questions were asked in the House of Commons regarding the trade in slaves, or so-called labourers, from the West Coast of Madagascar to Réunion and the activity of the slave-trade on the Mozambique Coast. Slave-owning in all parts under French authority was abolished by proclamation on September 27, 1896. Forced labour in the public service was abolished in 1901, but the personal tax due from 16 to 60 years has been very heavily increased.

Although there were notable French Abolitionists and Emancipators from the time of the French Revolution onwards, it was not until 1865 that the French Anti-Slavery Society was formed. An important Conference was held in Paris in 1867, convened by the French, British and Spanish Societies, and thenceforward French Abolitionists did all in their power to assist their Spanish colleagues in their uphill task. Cardinal Lavigerie, Archbishop of Algiers, played an outstanding part in rousing the Catholic Church in all parts of the world to the abominations of slave-owning and slave-trading. He spoke with magnificent eloquence and force at a great meeting held in London in 1888, and presented to the Society, through Cardinal Manning, a generous gift of 50,000 francs, part of a sum of 300,000 francs entrusted to him by the Pope for Anti-Slavery work. Cardinal Manning was a great supporter of the Anti-Slavery cause in this country, and did much to stimulate public opinion.

When the Victorian era opened, Spain was no longer a great Colonial Power and the main efforts of the Emancipators were concentrated on Porto Rico and Cuba. A Spanish Anti-Slavery Society was formed in 1865, Spanish Abolitionists attended the Paris Anti-Slavery Conference in 1867, Joseph Cooper, the Secretary of the British Society, visited Spain in 1868, and in the following year he received a striking letter from Garibaldi denouncing Spanish slavery. In 1870 the first step was taken by a decree declaring all slave children born after the passing of the Act free, under conditions. In 1873 a law was passed to abolish slavery in Porto Rico within three years, and in 1875 the British Society urged Lord Derby, then Prime Minister, to stipulate for the abolition of slavery before recognising Don Alfonso as King. It was at this time that Señor Vizcarrondo, the courageous Secretary of the Spanish Society, suffered imprisonment for his opinions.

Abolition in Cuba was a long and difficult business. In 1850 the Slave Trade was admittedly increasing, and in 1860 Lord John Russell acknowledged that between 30,000 and 40,000 African slaves were carried annually to Cuba. To the abominations of African slave-trading were added the iniquities of Chinese immigration on a large scale. The subject was brought up several times in Parliament from the year 1856 onwards, and in 1879 Lord Selborne, in the House of Lords, raised the whole question of slavery in Cuba and of our treaties with Spain, which gave us a right to demand emancipation. In 1885 the Anti-Slavery Society was able to report that 'Emancipation progressed steadily,' and in the following year slavery was finally abolished in Cuba, without any pecuniary indemnity to the owners—a real triumph for the Anti-Slavery Societies of Great Britain and Spain which had struggled long and earnestly to create public opinion.

The story of British efforts to get slave-trading and slave-owning abolished in Portuguese possessions is like that of the mouse in 'Alice in Wonderland'—'a long tale and a sad one,' and long before its ending the student of Anti-Slavery records finds himself murmuring with Alice, 'that was the fifth bend'—so many are the twists, evasions and disguises, so wearisome the contrast between the high-sounding moral phrases of Portuguese legislation and the 'patent continuance in evil-doing.' Our 'Ancient Ally' continued to indulge in slave-trading regardless of treaty obligations. In 1885 the Anti-Slavery Society reported that 'the Slave-trading practices of the Portuguese in their Colonies in Western Africa were notorious,' and in 1891 that 'sad accounts were received from West Africa of the enforced labour traffic carried on by the Portuguese Government.' The abolition of slavery in the Portuguese Island of Cape Verde was decreed by the Portuguese Government in 1874, and in

1875 another decree was issued putting an end to slavery in all Portuguese possessions within one year. But its legal termination was followed by various forms of disguised slavery in the Portuguese Cocoa Islands and Angola, as set forth in a later chapter.

Reference has already been made to the immense numbers of African slaves imported into Brazil in the years 1829–30. In 1840 the British Society circulated 8,000 pamphlets in Brazil and received a good deal of local support. In 1851 a local Anti-Slavery Society was formed. The Brazilian Government had in 1850 issued a decree declaring slave-trading to be piracy and signed a Slave Trade Convention with Great Britain. Brazilian Ministers seem honestly to have tried to observe their engagements, but they had against them a ring of rich and powerful Portuguese slave-traders and their own power over a loose confederation of provinces with an interminable coast line was limited and ineffectual. It must be confessed with no little shame that British mining companies in Brazil owned slaves, a fact to which the British Anti-Slavery Society drew repeated attention from 1859 until 1882, when the Final Court of Appeal granted judgment against the St. John D'el Rey Mining Company, and declared the slaves free after the Superintendent of the Company had been dismissed from the British Vice-Consulship which he held! The total abolition of slavery in Brazil took place in 1888, and for this no small credit was due to the Brazilian Anti-Slavery leader, Senator Nabuco.

Holland, as an important Colonial Power, was concerned in the slavery question. In 1854 her Government set up a Royal Commission on slavery in the Dutch Colonies, one of the Commissioners being a corresponding member of the British Anti-Slavery Society. In the following year the Society sent a deputation to Holland. British subjects were not guiltless, and in 1860 Lord John Russell instructed our Consul in Surinam to warn British subjects that the British Government intended to enforce the law against the Slave Trade. Victory was won in 1862 when Holland decreed total Emancipation to take place in her West Indian Colonies on July 1, 1863.

Scandinavian countries have always led the way in good works, so it is not surprising to find that Sweden, which had been one of the first to abolish the Slave Trade, abolished slave-owning in 1847, and that Denmark followed suit in all her Colonies in 1848. Russia has never been a Colonial Power, but it is interesting to note that the British Anti-Slavery Society addressed the Czar on the subject of serfdom in 1858 and that the serfs were emancipated in 1861. In 1873 Russia abolished slavery unconditionally in Khiva.

Germany did not enter the field as a Colonial Power until slave-trading and slave-owning had ceased to be reputable institutions. In 1871 the British Anti-Slavery Society corresponded with friends in Germany with the purpose of urging their co-operation with England in suppressing the East African Slave Trade, and twenty years later, a deputation from the Society on the same subject was sympathetically received by the Emperor William II at Buckingham Palace. During the same year the Slave Trade in Togoland was debated in the German Reichstag, but the Government denied the allegations made and stated that the domestic slavery which existed was not of a burdensome character and moreover formed the economic basis upon which the country was founded.

Turkey, Egypt and the Sudan require a volume to themselves, but can only be treated briefly. The refusal of Beaconsfield and Salisbury to take advantage of the opportunity offered by the Congress of Berlin in 1878 was bitterly regretted by the Anti-Slavery Society's supporters, whose Journal for August, 1878, remarked that:

> While England has taken on herself the most formidable responsibilities to sustain the remnant of Ottoman Rule, she has left Slavery and the Slave Trade, the prolific source of its crimes, its degradations and disorders, to flourish as before, when her word would have obtained, from an approving Congress, the adoption of measures for their final extinction.

Public feeling in England was aroused. Lord Shaftesbury stated that in Turkey the slaves were bought and sold extensively by private agents, and emphasised the point that as Turkish society was constituted, slavery was 'as necessary and indispensable to the Empire, especially among the wealthier classes, as the Sultan himself.' There was much evidence as to the regular slave trade in Circassian girls, carried on 'for the benefit of the luxurious and wealthy classes,' and the kidnapping and sale of white children was not uncommon. A petition from the Society was presented to the House of Lords, deploring the abandonment at the Berlin Congress of the British policy of opposition to slavery and the Slave Trade, and praying that the Turkish flag might no longer be suffered to protect the Slave Trade in East Africa. Egypt supplied many of the slaves required for Turkey. So did Tripoli. In 1893 the Italian Anti-Slavery Society reported that Turkish vessels carried slaves surreptitiously to various ports in the Levant, the authorities providing the traders with letters of liberation to cover the deception. The attention of Lord Rosebery, then Foreign Secretary, was called to the fraud, for Turkey had been one of the Powers to sign the Brussels Act in 1890. When Cyprus, after the Congress of Berlin, became a part of the British Empire, a discussion was raised in the House of Lords by Lord Shaftesbury. The answer given was that no slavery existed in the island, and that if the law were honestly enforced in Turkey (which was admitted to be a very rare occurrence) it would not exist there either.

Slave-trading and slave-owning in Egypt and the Sudan occupied British reformers for many years. In 1867 the British and French Anti-Slavery Societies went on a deputation to Ismail Pasha, Khedive of Egypt, on the question of the White Nile Slave Trade.

In 1873, Ismail [1] invited General Gordon to become Governor of the Equatorial Province (of the Sudan) in succession to Sir Samuel Baker. Gordon was attracted by the prospect of opening up these distant lands to legitimate commerce and thus striking a blow at the slave-trade, and he accepted the Khedive's offer. For three years (1874–76) he was engaged . . . . in one unceasing struggle with a deadly climate . . . and a corrupt native administration. All but one of the white colleagues whom he took with him either died or were invalided home, and he was left, practically single-handed, to carry out the arduous task of establishing a line of posts along the reaches of the Upper Nile right through to the Lakes. He succeeded and the Khedive made him Governor-General of the whole Sudan, an area of a million square miles.

[1] Dr. Bernard Allen, *Observer*, January 22, 1933.

For three years (1877–79) he ruled this huge province with hardly any European assistance and by a ruthless suppression of corrupt officials, strict enforcement of justice and merciless severity against the slave-dealers, inaugurated a reign of order and fair dealing that won him the affection of the people. . . . On one well-known occasion when some desperate slave-dealers were threatening revolt, he dashed across country on his camel, rode with the smallest of escorts into a camp where thousands of armed ruffians were assembled, and cowed them into submission by sheer force of his personality. Courage counts for much in the East, and the hold which Gordon gained over the Soudanese people was due to his daring actions as well as to his beneficent rule.

After Gordon left, the slave-dealers began again to raise their heads, and in 1881 the Mahdi's successful revolt broke out in the Sudan (at almost the same time as Arabi's revolt in Egypt). Gordon was asked by the Gladstone Ministry to undertake the perilous task of withdrawing many thousands of defeated Egyptian soldiers from the Sudan. The story of his heroic death on January 26, 1885, at Khartoum is well known. He was described by Sir Henry Jackson as 'A soldier by profession, a philanthropist by inclination, a ruler and leader of men by nature. . . . He aspires to govern men for their good and has uniformly and conspicuously succeeded.' He was a warm supporter of the Anti-Slavery Society, corresponded frequently when abroad and met their Committee when in England, and wrote of their work, which he liberally supported :

the Anti-Slavery Society has probably done more than any one religious society in the world for the releasing of the bonds of man from the cruelty of his fellow-creatures. Unsectarian, and appealing to the sentiments of humanity in every man, no civilised being ought to exist who has not some interest in its success.

After the fall of Arabi and the occupation of the country by British forces, the British Government became virtually responsible for the government of Egypt ; and to Sir Evelyn Baring (later Lord Cromer) belongs the main credit for suppressing slave-trading and slave-owning in Egypt. Thanks to his efforts the Anti-Slavery Convention of 1877 between Egypt and Great Britain ceased to be a dead letter, and in 1891 he was able to report to Parliament that it had been found an efficient instrument for the gradual suppression of slavery, and that thanks to the Slave-Trade Department under Colonel Schaefer, the trade was said to be extinct, although in 1894 he was obliged to note that continual vigilance was necessary to prevent the smuggling in of the slaves from the west and to control the shipment of slaves from the coast south of Suakin. Lord Cromer's Report for 1898 proved the success attained by his efforts. Although, despite the utmost vigilance, a few cases of slave-trading still occurred, domestic slavery in Egypt proper was rapidly disappearing and infractions of the law were reported by the people, a sure proof of the support of public opinion.

General Gordon and Lord Cromer, though their spheres and methods differed widely, were both in their different ways admirable examples of what can be accomplished by first-class administration and energy.

Among the South American countries progress was made, though it is to be feared that accomplishment often lagged behind promise. Chili decreed the

Slave Trade to be piracy as early as 1841. Argentine 'constitutionally abolished' slavery in 1853, Peru decreed the 'unconditional abolition of slavery' in 1854, but she followed the bad example of Queensland in setting up a new slave trade by importing Polynesian labourers who were slaves in everything but name. After the Anti-Slavery and Aborigines Protection Societies had presented a memorial to Lord John Russell in 1864, the British and Peruvian Governments took action and the traffic was forbidden. At another period Chinese coolies were imported, as they were also into Cuba and Mexico, under conditions of appalling cruelty.

From 1883 onwards the Anti-Slavery Society was greatly concerned with the open slave traffic and barbarous treatment of slaves in Morocco. The Secretary and Treasurer of the Society visited Morocco in 1884, when the first and last Anti-Slavery meeting ever held in Morocco took place in the house of a British resident, who formed a local Committee of European sympathisers. The British Minister, Sir J. Hay Drummond, described the country as 'An Augean stable beyond his power to cleanse.' The prisons were barbarous beyond description; men, women and children were sold in the streets like brute beasts; heart-breaking scenes might be witnessed any day in the slave markets of Morocco City and Fez, and glaring cases of cruelty were of almost daily occurrence. In 1887 Mr. Donald Mackenzie, on behalf of the Society, presented to the Sultan the first Anti-Slavery Address ever received by a Sovereign of Morocco. Mr. Mackenzie reported that, although Morocco was still a stronghold of slavery, the Society's efforts had already done much by securing the closing of the slave market in port towns and by interfering to prevent many cruelties. But alas, in 1891, local reports showed that public auction sales of slaves in the seaport towns had been resumed, and in the same year Lord Salisbury, in a notable speech at Glasgow, felt himself compelled to state that 'Morocco still remains the home of the worst abuses, of the greatest cruelty, of the greatest ignorance and backwardness in all that conduces to prosperity or humanity.'

In 1898, His Majesty's Minister at Tangier wrote to the Secretary of the Anti-Slavery Society that there were serious difficulties in the way of proposing with any hope of success any measures likely to lead to the suppression or mitigation of slavery.[1]

The Bey of Tunis abolished the Slave Trade in 1842, but this decree appears to have been ineffective until about 1877, when actual abolition was thankfully noted by the Anti-Slavery Society. A time-lag of thirty-five years between promise and performance is remarkably long, even in countries in which difficulties are great and procrastinations and delays inevitable!

Abyssinia is engaging so much attention to-day that it is interesting to find that in 1873 the Anti-Slavery Society sent an Address to Menelek, then 'King of Shoa,' asking him to stop slave caravans passing through his kingdom, and that in 1879 he sent 'the joyful message' that he had abolished the slave trade throughout the kingdom, and complained that he was excluded from all legitimate trade with other countries by the action of Egypt. 'Will you kindly raise your

[1] Morocco is still a field in which grave need for reform exists.—J. H.

powerful voice,' wrote Menelek, 'in order that I may have the way opened to me, for I desire to inaugurate in my Kingdom European civilisation, intelligence and art?'

Considerable difference of opinion was felt as to the success of the Liberian experiment as a practical solution for slavery. There were those who shared the misgivings expressed many years before by Clarkson when in a letter to William Lloyd Garrison, the American Emancipator, he wrote: 'Newly emancipated slaves are not qualified to become Colonists in Africa to any good purpose. How could they civilise others, who wanted civilising themselves? The American Colonisation Society had no right to send the scum of their population to Africa.' Clarkson's misgivings have been only too amply justified.

Thus it will be seen that fifty years after British Abolition, the British Foreign Office, the Abolitionists and the Emancipators were still struggling to obtain the abolition of the Slave Trade and the liberty of the slaves in a score of countries.

It is estimated that Great Britain spent £50,000,000 between 1817 and 1875 in naval efforts to put down slave-trading. The partial success obtained by these efforts was due to the fact that slave-trading could not be suppressed so long as slave-owning was permitted to exist.

The abolition of slavery as a recognised legal status in British possessions, after the great initial step had been taken in 1833, was fairly straightforward provided that the power of the Crown could be directly exercised. Where the British Government possessed only indirect rights, as in the Indian Native States and the Protectorates of Zanzibar and Sierra Leone, reform was a slow and difficult process.

Abolition in British India was the logical sequence to the Act of 1833. In 1840 the Anti-Slavery Society was busily agitating against slavery in British India, in the following year the Society brought the question before the British electors, and in 1843 abolition took place in the whole of British India 'under the same great Viceroy, Lord William Bentinck, to whom India owes the abolition of Suttee,' and in Scinde, but in most of the Native States slavery lingered for a good many years. The enlightened attitude of the Aborigines Protection Society towards Indian questions is interesting at the present day. The Society was pressing for the employment of Indian natives in positions of trust and responsibility as early as 1851. Its Report in 1856, the year before the Mutiny, contains the following warning: 'We have sometimes felt terrified in the contemplation of the policy of aggression and conquest which we have pursued in India. . . . It becomes the solemn duty of every English citizen to see that the Indian subjects of Queen Victoria participate, as far as circumstances will permit, in the rights and privileges of Englishmen.' Very shortly before the Mutiny broke out public attention was drawn to the torture and oppression practised by the Indian police, to the opium monopoly and to 'the few hundreds of thousands of pounds expended per annum for education and public works, whilst they are almost perpetually draining the resources of the country in external aggressive warfare.' The Society analysed the underlying causes of the Mutiny as the poverty of the vast masses of the population, police oppression, and the fact that 'Hindoos, having grown in intelligence and formed a true estimate of their strength and our weakness, no longer regard us as invincible conquerors.'

The views of the Protestant Missionaries in India, who presented a petition to the House of Commons through the Hon. Arthur Kinnaird very shortly before the Mutiny, were identical with those of the Society. When the Mutiny was over the humane instructions of Lord Canning, Governor-General of India, regarding the treatment of Indian mutineers, aroused the fury of *The Times*, the *Morning Post*, and a large majority of the Members of the House of Commons, but the Aborigines Protection Society assured him that 'neither he nor his children will ever have reason to be ashamed of the title of "Clemency Canning."'

In Ceylon and the Straits Settlements Abolition took place, as in India, in 1843. Hong Kong followed suit in 1844 with what our predecessors described optimistically as 'complete abolition.' It is to be feared they knew little or nothing of the old-established system of Mui Tsai or child slavery which is weighing so heavily upon our consciences to-day.

Zanzibar was not recognised by France and Germany as a British Protectorate until 1890, but our influence there had been growing ever since the death of the Sultan Seyyid Said in 1856, and our responsibility for the continuance of slavery and slave-trading on a large scale had been a matter of steadily increasing concern to the Anti-Slavery movement in Great Britain. In 1870 Mr. Gilpin, M.P., obtained the appointment of a Select Committee of the House of

Commons, and the following year Sir Bartle Frere was appointed by the British Government as a Special Anti-Slavery Commissioner in East Africa. He was succeeded by Sir John Kirk, and it was in his time that a young English missionary, Arthur West, bought from the Sultan of Zanzibar the slave market, giving his whole capital (of £100,000[1]) to do so. On Christmas Day, 1874, while Arthur West lay dying in Sir John Kirk's house at Zanzibar, the foundation of the present cathedral was laid on the site of the slave market.

In 1876 Sir John Kirk succeeded in getting the Sultan to promise to forbid the export of slaves, but in 1890 it was discovered that Zanzibar slaves were being enlisted under compulsion to serve in the Congo, although in that same year the Sultan had issued a decree abolishing the legal status of slavery. This decree was so manifestly a dead letter that in 1894 Mr. J. A. Pease (now Lord Gainford) raised the whole question of Abolition in the House of Commons. He was supported by Joseph Chamberlain, who denounced the Government for not taking this step, as well as for not building a railway and establishing our rule in the interior. Sir Charles Dilke opened another debate two months later, but progress was very slow. In 1895 a valuable step was taken by the Anti-Slavery Society which sent out Mr. Donald Mackenzie as a Special Commissioner to study slavery and slave-trading not only in Zanzibar but also in the Red Sea. His report was of great value, and after a petition from the Anti-Slavery Society, the Society of Friends and the Congregational Union, and several more debates

[1] *The Times*, December 24, 1932.

in Parliament, Sir Edward Grey admitted on behalf of the Government that 'the thing had to be done,' and Sir William Harcourt added 'at the earliest possible moment.'

This long-continued pressure produced at last, in 1897, a decree signed by the Sultan of Zanzibar for the abolition of the legal status of slavery, but even after this important measure progress was exceedingly slow.

Even our own representative in Zanzibar, Sir Arthur Hardinge, aroused considerable anxiety amongst reformers in this country by his despatches defending slavery and estimating the financial loss to the revenue which he anticipated from its abolition, and still more by his appeal on behalf of the slave *holders* to 'English justice.'

Progress continued to be very slow up to the end of Queen Victoria's reign, but it must be remembered that the traditions and customs of Zanzibar were entirely opposed to reform, and that the lack of enlightened local public opinion made the suppression of slave-trading and slave-owning an exceptionally difficult task. That it was at last achieved was almost entirely due to pressure from this country.

CHAPTER IX

Victorian Struggles

Boer *versus* Native—The Basutos—The Bechuana—Tucker in Uganda—Kaffir Wars—Kanaka Labour—Scandal of New Hebrides—Polynesian Kidnapping.

There are few bright spots in the history of the treatment of native races in South Africa during the Victorian era. But amongst these are the restoration to the Kaffirs in 1840, through Lord Glenelg and thanks to Buxton's intervention, of the Adelaide Territory. Another bright spot is the wise administration of Basutoland since 1884. But taken as a whole, it is a record in which there is little cause for pride, and much for regret. The South African attitude to natives was admirably described by Lord Bryce in 1897 in his masterly 'Impressions of South Africa':

> Unluckily South Africa was colonised in the 17th Century, when the importation of negro slaves was deemed the easiest means of securing cheap and abundant labour. From 1658 to 1834 . . . it was to slaves that the hardest and humblest kinds of work were allotted. The white people lost the habit of performing manual toil and acquired the habit of despising it. . . . Thus, when at last slavery was abolished, the custom of leaving menial labour or toilsome work to people of colour continued as strong as ever. It is as strong as ever to-day.

Lord Olivier said the same thing in different words

in 1927.[1] 'South Africa is, in short, in the singular situation, in the British Commonwealth of Nations, in the Community of Christendom, and practically in the whole of the civilized world, of being still a slave state.'

It is little wonder that the Dutch farmers resented deeply the Emancipation Act of 1834. Their share (about £3,000,000) of the sum of £20,000,000 paid in compensation to the owners throughout the British Colonies was felt by them to be quite inadequate. Their labour difficulties became acute, labour in many districts becoming so scarce that agriculture could hardly be carried on. They had already been hotly indignant at the Governmental Ordinance of 1828 which placed them on an equal footing with Hottentots and other free coloured people as regards civil rights, and they had bitterly resented the restoration of the Adelaide Territory, so recently conquered by themselves, to the Kaffirs. When slavery was abolished on grounds which they could neither understand nor approve, it was more than they could endure, and there followed the famous Great Trek of the Dutch Boers, which began in 1836, northwards to the unsettled districts later to be known as the Orange Free State and the Transvaal.

Bryce remarks with fine insight that 'the emigrants seem all through to have treated the natives much as Israel treated the natives of Canaan and to have conceived themselves to have Old Testament authority for occupying the territories of the heathen and reducing them by the sternest methods to serfdom or submission.' This Biblical attitude was demonstrated

[1] Lord Olivier, *The Anatomy of African Misery.*

by the Boer Commandant, quoted by Buxton, who found it inconceivable that Providence should permit 'the Heathen' to possess such magnificent herds of fine cattle, and acted on the assumption!

The British Parliament might decree the abolition of slavery, but the Boers continued to hold the native races in a condition of servitude, although—when the Transvaal and the Orange Free State emerged, as free Republics, from the Rand River Convention of 1852 and the Bloemfontein Convention of 1853—the Boers undertook in both Conventions to permit neither slave-owning nor slave-trading. But the reports of missionaries and the records of the Anti-Slavery and Aborigines Protection Societies continued for many years afterwards to contain evidence of the virtual enslavement and ill-treatment of the natives.

> For a good while after they settled in the Transvaal the Boers had a system of apprenticing Kaffir children which was with difficulty distinguishable from predial serfdom; and though they have constantly denied that they sanctioned either the kidnapping of children or the treatment of the apprentices as slaves, there is good reason to think that in some parts of the country these abuses did exist.[1]

Not only did they continue a system scarcely distinguishable from slave-owning, but they also carried on what can only be described as slave-raiding.

The records of the Aborigines Protection Society contain frequent allusions to raids undertaken, sometimes in retaliation, sometimes out of mere aggression, by the Boers into native territories, from which the spoils were not only cattle, but women slaves and child

[1] Bryce, *Impressions of South Africa.*

slaves. Livingstone has told how, in 1852, he recognised on farms in the Transvaal Kaffir children held as slaves who had been carried off by the Boers under Pretorius from his Mission Settlement.

But cruelty to natives has not been confined to the Dutch Boers, for Bryce describes how 'a few years ago, in the eastern province, a white farmer—an Englishman and not a Boer—flogged his Kaffir servant so severely, that the latter died; and when the culprit was put on his trial, and acquitted by a white jury, his white neighbours escorted him home with a band of music.' An almost exact parallel to many similar incidents in the West Indies before emancipation and even during the four years of apprenticeship.

A common and long-continued practice, especially on the borders of civilisation, has been for many years to provoke native servants by ill-usage to run away before the day of payment arrives.

The saddest and most sinister fact—one of even greater import than isolated cruelties—in the whole history of South Africa, even to the present day, is the attitude of white towards black. Bryce remarks that 'The traveller in South Africa is astonished at the strong feeling of dislike and contempt—one might almost say, of hostility—which the bulk of the whites show to their black neighbours.' Bryce analyses it as springing

partly from the old feeling of contempt for the slaves . . . from physical aversion . . . from incompatibility of character and temper. . . . The sense of his superior intelligence and energy of will produces in the European a sort of tyrannous spirit . . . the attitude of contempt is stronger among the Dutch than among the English. But the English also have done so many things to regret that it does not lie with them to cast stones at the Boers. . . . And the mildness of Colonial Law (i.e. Cape Colony as compared with Transvaal and Orange Free State) is largely due to the influence of the Home Government and to that recognition of the equal civil rights of all subjects which has long pervaded the common law of England.

The difference between Boer and British on the question of equal rights for black and white is fundamental. The Grondwet (fundamental law) of the Transvaal Republic declared, in 1858, and declares to-day, that '*the people will suffer no equality of whites and blacks, either in state or in church.*'

It is possible to feel both admiration and sympathy for the sturdy spirit which impelled the Boer settlers to make the Great Trek, and yet to deplore their attitude towards native races and to see in it the seeds of even graver troubles in the future.

One of the brightest examples of British administration, not only in South Africa but throughout the Empire, is Basutoland, where Moshesh, the great native chief, prayed on his death-bed that his nation might ever rest under the security of the Union Jack.

Government policy towards the natives has always been far more enlightened in the Cape than in the Boer States, but it is to Basutoland that we must turn if we wish to find a part of South Africa in which the Kaffirs really have a 'look-in.' In the words of Lord Bryce,[1] 'Basutoland is the Switzerland of South Africa,' and very appropriately is the part of South Africa where the old inhabitants, defended by their hills, have retained the largest measure of freedom. This freedom

[1] Bryce, *Impressions of South Africa.*

they owe largely to the famous Moshesh, who built up his power from small beginnings in about 1824 and ruled them until he died in 1871. Many were the wars which he had to sustain with the native tribes who lived round him, as well as with the white settlers. In 1852 Sir George Cathcart, one of the less wise Governors of Cape Colony, led 5,000 British infantry and 500 cavalry, besides artillery, against the Basutos, and after considerable fighting found his force in great danger and set out to retire to the Caledon River.

But Moshesh knew the real strength of the British, though he had been driven into the war by the over-confidence of his people and their unwillingness to pay the cattle fine which the Government had demanded, and after consulting one of the French missionaries of the Paris Evangelical Society, he begged Sir George Cathcart for peace, declaring that he would do all he could to keep his tribesmen in order. Thereafter he 'enjoyed the fame of being the only native potentate who had come out of a struggle with Great Britain virtually if not formally the victor.' [1]

In 1865 Moshesh and his people were again engaged in war, this time with the Orange Free State, which had found the Basutos troublesome neighbours. The Free State Militia were skilled in native warfare, and Moshesh, finding himself likely to be overpowered, besought the Imperial Government to receive him and his people 'under the large folds of the flag of England.' His request was granted; the High Commissioner declared the Basutos to be thenceforth British subjects, and in 1871 they came under the administrative control of Cape Colony. Moshesh died soon after, leaving a

[1] Bryce, *Impressions of South Africa.*

name which, in the words of Lord Bryce, 'has become famous in South Africa.' He was one of the remarkable instances, like Toussaint l'Ouverture and the Hawaian King, Ramehameha the First, of a man, sprung from a savage race, who effected great things by a display of wholly exceptional gifts. His sayings have become proverbs in native mouths. One of them is worth noting as a piece of grim humour, a quality rare among the Kaffirs. Some of his chief men had been urging him, after he had become powerful, to take vengeance upon certain cannibals who were believed to have killed and eaten his grandparents. Moshesh said: 'I must consider well before I disturb the sepulchres of my ancestors.'

Though he never became a Christian he supported Christianity. In 1833 he welcomed the missionaries of the Paris Evangelical Society and gave them land. He found their counsels of infinite value in the troublous times that followed and he never ceased to protect and encourage them. He listened, like many Kaffir chiefs, to sermons, and enjoyed the society of his French friends, who with his encouragement laid so well and surely the foundations of their religion that, as Bryce wrote in 1897, 'Nowhere has the Gospel made such progress among the Kaffirs as in Basutoland.' [1]

After the death of Moshesh, Basutoland remained quiet until 1879, when the Cape Government, urged, it seems, by Sir Bartle Frere, then Governor of Cape Colony, conceived the unwise project of disarming the Basutos. The Cape Prime Minister, who met them in their great popular assembly, the Pitso, was warned by their chiefs that any attempt to enforce disarma-

[1] This holds true to this day.—J. H.

ment would meet with resistance. The Aborigines Protection Society in London, though a body of markedly pacifist tendencies, pressed the view that while no doubt it was a pity that so many Basutos possessed firearms, it would be far better to let them keep their weapons than to provoke war. Unfortunately rash counsels won the day, war followed, and the Basutos gave the Colonial troops so much trouble that the Cape Government contemplated abandoning the territory altogether.

General Gordon was invited by Mr. Scanlen, the Cape Premier, to advise his Government as to their future policy in regard to Basutoland. Gordon arrived in May, 1883, and soon came to the conclusion that the trouble could easily be settled if the Cape Ministry would give the Basutos a reasonable measure of self-government through their own chiefs. He was unfavourably impressed by the lack of tact, sympathy and capacity to deal with native races shown by a good many of the European magistrates who administered the territory. He told the Cape Government plainly that they ought to arrive at a settlement with the Basutos, and that he would not fight against a people whose cause he believed to be just. His advice was accepted, and Sir Hercules Robinson, the High Commissioner, in the Speech from the Throne to the Cape Legislature in 1883, stated that the Government did not propose in future to interfere with the internal affairs of Basutoland, though they would control its external relations.

In 1884 the Imperial Government took over from the Cape Government the oversight of the administration, and by their sympathetic supervision and advice have knit Basutoland to Britain. From that day there has been a resident British Commissioner who advises the Basuto chiefs (most of whom are descendants of the great Moshesh) who preside over the districts and wards into which the country is divided. Bryce wrote: 'The British authorities interfere as little as may be with native ways, trusting to time, peace, education, and the missionaries to civilise the people.'

Once a year the Commissioner meets the whole people in their National Assembly called the Pitso. The Paramount Chief presides, but all freemen, gentle and simple, have a right to speak in it. The shorthand report of the great Pitso held in 1879, at which the question of disarmament was brought forward by the Cape Minister, is of great interest, as showing the freedom and intelligence with which the speakers expressed their views. One speaker commented with severity upon an unfortunate phrase lately used at Cape Town by a member of the Cape Government: 'Mr. U. said the Basutos were the natural enemies of the white men because we were black. Is that language which should be used by a high officer of the Government? Let sentiments like these pass away—we are being educated to believe that all people are equal and feel that sentiments like these are utterly wrong.'

Bryce describes the great progress made by education—250 schools, all but two of which were, in his time, conducted by the missionaries—French-Protestant, Roman Catholic and English Episcopalian. By 1924 there were 522 native elementary schools besides normal and industrial schools, proving that the Basutos have kept up their zeal for education. Bryce comments significantly on the belief of the people in the goodwill of the Government, and adds that

> So far, the experiment of leaving a native race to advance in their own way, under their own Chiefs, but carefully supervised by imperial officers, has proved successful. . . . Whoever feels for the native and cares for his future must wish a fair chance for the experiment that is now being tried in Basutoland, of letting him develop in his own way, shielded from the rude pressure of the white man.

One other bright spot is the Bechuanaland Protectorate, not unlike that of Basutoland in its administration, and here, also, the natives are assisted to develop on their own lines. In these two countries in which the native has freedom to develop in his own way, under the wise guidance and advice of British officials, his progress in education and civilisation has been remarkable. To find another parallel (though one differing in certain respects) we must go to another part of Africa. Uganda, which, after having been administered for some years by the British East African Company, was declared a British Protectorate in 1894. It is now under direct administration, but the native kings or chiefs are encouraged to conduct the government of their own subjects. The province of Buganda is recognised as a native kingdom. Its intelligent and civilised people were first converted by English and French missionaries. Alexander Mackay was one of the pioneers and another was Bishop Hannington, who was put to death in 1885 by the weak and cruel king Mwanga. Hannington's murder was followed by the martyrdom of hundreds of native Christians, thirty of whom were publicly burnt at Mengo. Like the English bishops, they 'lit a candle' which has never been extinguished.

In 1890 the Rev. Alfred R. Tucker became Bishop of Uganda. His magnificent work as a missionary was only equalled by his practical statesmanship in assisting the political and economic development of Uganda, and by his championship of native interests. He opposed slavery tooth and nail and did much to secure its abolition in the Sultanate of Zanzibar. When home on leave in 1897 he attended a Conference organised by the Anti-Slavery Society and protested against orders issued by H.M. Commissioner giving masters permission to search the mission stations on the mainland for runaway slaves and to claim their surrender. Not content with protest, the bishop defended a fugitive slave-girl in Mombasa, and himself conducted her case. The court decided that the girl could not claim her freedom as a fugitive slave. But there is little doubt that the indignation aroused in England by this and similar cases had valuable results in hastening the slow process of suppressing slavery in East Africa, to which reference has already been made.

Basutoland, Bechuanaland and Uganda have one striking thing in common. Left to their freedom they have each produced rulers who have developed a measure of real statecraft which in each case has, with the helpful advice of sympathetic Europeans, carried the progress of their countries forward at a pace not less rapid than European States at similar periods in their own history.

Thanks to what has been, on the whole, an enlightened policy on the part of the Colonial Office, the natives of the Cape possessed equal civil rights and a limited franchise throughout Queen Victoria's reign, and have in general received much better treatment and greater opportunities for progress and education than in the Boer States. But the attitude towards natives of the majority of the English settlers in the Cape differed, particularly in the early days, little, if at all, from that of the Boers, and the protests of the Anti-Slavery and Aborigines Protection Societies were violently resented. An amusing example of the abuse to which they were subjected is to be found in the *Cape of Good Hope Observer* of 1851, which describes them as 'these Saints and Aboriginal Society men, these ignorant meddling maw-worms.'

The attitude of the 'maw-worms' to the series of Kaffir wars which took place between the years 1834 and 1852 showed a great deal more practical statesmanship than was displayed by the men on the spot. As a speaker expressed it in the House of Commons in 1851: 'These wars arose out of the encroachments of the settlers upon the lands of the natives, and the wholesale annexation of extensive tracts of country.' [1] Sir E. N. Buxton, in the same debate, showed that if the principles laid down in Lord Glenelg's famous despatch with regard to the restoration of the Adelaide Territory had been accepted as the basis of our future policy from that time, we should have been saved the sacrifice of life and treasure which had ensued from the Kaffir wars. He lamented that Glenelg's policy had not been carried on and denied, in answer to Gladstone, that it had failed. So far from our surrender to the Kaffirs of the Adelaide Territory

[1] Speech by Sir William Molesworth, M.P., House of Commons, April 10, 1851.

having been regarded by them as an act of weakness, they considered it only an act of simple justice. During the time that Sir Andreas Stockenström, carrying on the Glenelg system, administered the Kat River Territory, perfect security, tranquillity and contentment had prevailed.

The annexation system, on the other hand, resulted in a succession of wars which entailed the expenditure of at least £4,000,000. As a contemporary writer in South Africa observed: 'The Grahamstown Journal called it a *concession* to leave the Kaffirs their independence up to the Kei. That is a novel adaptation of the word.' Their lands, their wealth, their independence were taken from them and the smallest favours were then called concessions. No wonder they revolted. But by the end of 1853 they were broken and almost starving.

In 1855 British policy took a turn for the better, when General Cathcart (whose Minute on the Kaffir Wars was described by the Aborigines Protection Society as 'an unfair record against a feeble and crushed race') was replaced by Sir George Grey, who had already won fame by his wise and generous treatment of the Maoris, and whose enlightened policy during his four years' term of office achieved remarkable success. He treated the natives with justice, established schools, encouraged missionaries, fed the starving Kaffirs, and won the confidence of Moshesh. He was not sent out until much irreparable mischief had been done, but his four years' term of office is a remarkable instance of what an enlightened Governor can accomplish.

The Zulu War of 1879 is remembered more for the

sad death of the young Prince Imperial at the battle of Isandlhana than for the causes that led up to it—yet these deserve study to-day. The British in Natal had serious provocation, but it was the opinion of the Aborigines Protection Society, as expressed in 1879, that 'It is almost a waste of time to discuss the nominal causes of the war when we know that it is only being prosecuted in order to break up the military organisation of the Zulus and make their country a British dependency.' The Report went on to say truly that 'In all South African Wars the land invariably plays a prominent part,' a truism which hardly needs to be laboured.

One of the sternest fights waged in the Victorian era on behalf of native races was against Kanaka contract labour from the Polynesian Islands. This was a particularly sordid method of obtaining cheap native labour from a distance by fraudulent means, and ill-using it when so obtained. Where it differed from the African slave trade was in the fact that the labourers were taken from their islands under a nominal contract, under engagements for nominally limited periods, to countries in which slavery was illegal. The South Sea Islands were the happy hunting ground of disreputable adventurers of several nationalities who took the unfortunate islanders on board sometimes by sheer kidnapping, sometimes by pseudo-contract. Originally started by the Peruvians, it was carried on by English, French, Germans and Austrians to obtain cheap labour for the cultivation of cotton, sugar and other tropical produce in the South Seas.

It seems to have been commenced somewhere about

1850. An early record[1] states that in 1858 Kingsmill Islanders were kidnapped by a Frenchman and taken to Réunion, where they were sold to the planters as so-called 'immigrants.'

In 1860 the Aborigines Protection Society persuaded Lord John Russell to protest against the kidnapping of Polynesian Islanders by Peruvian citizens for the mines and guano islands of Peru, where they were treated with atrocious cruelty. Russell protested to the Peruvian Minister, who said that his Government had abandoned the trade and would return the so-called immigrants to their islands. How much that undertaking was worth may be gauged by the fact that in 1866 the missionaries of the London Missionary Society in Samoa informed the Aborigines Protection Society that islanders were still being kidnapped and shipped to Peru. But while the British Government was addressing protests to Peru, British subjects in Australia were doing the same thing. In 1867 the Hon. Robert Toms, member of the Legislative Council of New South Wales and owner of a cotton plantation in Queensland, was engaged, with others, in the import and employment of Kanaka labourers, who were admittedly obtained by fraudulent means, quite unprotected, ill-treated and only paid (and then only in goods) at the end of three years. Naval officers on the spot used strong language to the Colonial Office, and Captain J. P. Luce, R.N., Senior Naval Officer on the Australian station, made a spirited protest in a letter to Sir George Bowen, Governor of Queensland. The Aborigines Protection Society presented a memorial to the Duke of Buckingham, then Colonial Secretary,

[1] *Journal of Aborigines Protection Society*, 1858.

asking 'with what consistency can the Mother country rebuke Peruvians for kidnapping Polynesians, if her own subjects . . . engage in a similar pursuit?'

In 1869 a deputation waited on Earl Granville, who had succeeded the Duke of Buckingham at the Colonial Office, when Mr. Charles Buxton, M.P., as chief spokesman, showed himself a worthy son of his father by his able protests. Kidnapping on a large scale continued to be carried on and the English reformers urged that the introduction of Polynesian labour into Queensland ought never to have been permitted by Sir George Bowen, whose attitude appears to have been that the alleged kidnapping and other abuses and cruelties did not exist, and that the Queensland planters must have the labour.

The Queensland Legislature had already passed an Act to regulate the conditions of the traffic, but it was not observed. A letter in 1870 from the Rev. John G. Paton, Presbyterian Minister at the Polynesian Island of Aniwa, described how an old chief who used to be friendly 'informed us that his people were nearly all taken away in man-stealing vessels.' Paton stated that natives had been carried off by the thousand lately, that not one man in the trade had complied with the conditions of the Queensland Act, and asked:

> How can the Queensland Government sanction and protect this horrid trade in human beings with all its crime and bloodshed? The complaints of natives regarding their friends are heartrending. Some are surprised, bound and carried off by force. Others are got on board under every artifice and deception by the agents of the vessels, who are generally adepts at deceiving. . . . Some are represented as going ashore in the garb of a missionary, Bible in hand.

In a deputation to the Earl of Kimberley, Colonial

Secretary, Mr. P. A. Taylor, M.P., described the so-called immigration as 'nothing better than a compound of piracy and slave-trading similar to that which we have put down in connection with the Peruvian Government.' Kimberley sent a very strongly worded protest to the Governor of Queensland, and the Queenslanders were highly indignant against the Aborigines Protection Society.

In 1871 England was deeply stirred by the news of the murder of Bishop Patteson. He was beloved by all, and it was said of him by the missionaries that 'he knew no difference of denominations. It was enough for him that they were doing their Master's work,' while the islanders loved and trusted him throughout the Pacific. Not long before his death he described how some of the traders, with devilish cunning, had painted their ship white in exact imitation of his own ship *The Southern Cross* and sent one of their number ashore dressed like a missionary, to tell the natives that the Bishop was on board with a broken leg and they must come off and see him. Once on board, the natives were clapped into the hold and the ship sailed. Several cargoes were obtained in this atrocious manner. Then one day the Bishop came himself in *The Southern Cross* to one of the islands whose inhabitants had been tricked in this way; and thinking that he was come to steal them away again, they murdered him, their best friend.

His death was largely responsible for the Pacific Islanders Protection Bill introduced by Lord Kimberley. But alas! the excellent intentions of Parliament in passing this Act were in practice frustrated. Lord Carnarvon, one of the most enlightened Colonial

Secretaries towards Kaffirs and Polynesian Islanders alike, described the traffic in 1874 as 'very shocking,' and added that 'as a Government we have it most distinctly at heart to do everything within our power to suppress this traffic, believing . . . that it is in many respects a mere carrying on of a slave-trade of a very heinous and atrocious character.' The Bishop of Lichfield said that 'the people who conduct the labour traffic have lately taken to buying young boys and paying for them just as if they were pigs,' facts vouched for by Mr. A. W. Davidson, the Queensland correspondent of the Aborigines Protection Society. Another correspondent wrote to the *Scotsman* that

> the Islanders are engaged for three years at £6 per year but never get it, only, after 3 years, a box containing a few articles such as a jew's harp, a piece of calico, etc. They are insufficiently fed . . . kicked and knocked about. Their treatment is a disgrace to humanity. . . . I could tell you of cruelties that would make your blood run cold. The planters will not engage white men if they can get black, although sugar-growing pays quite well with white labour.

The languages of the various islands from which they were brought were not understood in Queensland, thus the labour contracts which the labourers were supposed to have signed meant, to them, nothing at all.

In 1877 a Government Committee which had been set up to enquire into Polynesian labour in Queensland issued its report,[1] which whitewashed the local Govern-

[1] Queensland had also a bad record in its treatment of aborigines, and in 1875 a Royal Commission was appointed to enquire into their condition, which made certain useful recommendations for official Protectors, land reserves, the prohibition of the sale of drink, and for medical assistance, education and Christian teaching.

ment and actually administered a snub to Mr. Sheridan, the Protector of Native Labour, for making the obviously just proposal that the evidence of the islanders should be admissible in the Courts of Law.

In 1878 the labour position in Queensland was considerably changed by the influx of 20,000 Chinese, caused by discoveries of gold. The colonists, becoming afraid of being elbowed out, then imposed a tax of £10 per head on every Chinaman, besides other taxes, including 1*d.* a lb. on their rice. The opponents of Kanaka labour enquired why Queensland, which had led the way in the traffic in Kanaka labour, complained when so abundantly supplied with Chinese labour! In 1883 the supply of labour was further increased by the import of indentured labourers from India and Ceylon. But the import of Kanaka labourers continued and serious and well-authenticated complaints as to their treatment and the manner in which they were obtained were made to successive Colonial Secretaries.

The Rev. J. G. Paton wrote: 'the Kanaka labour traffic is a trade in men and women. . . . Wherever they can find a market for these Islanders thither they are carried to be engaged, or rather to be "sold," at so much per head, according to age and strength. Some few pass into domestic service, where they are not so badly treated, but the great bulk of them go to the sugar plantations, where there is little before them but thinly veiled slavery.' Paton went on to say of the labour system:

> The only visible advantage that has ever accrued from it has been the enrichment of the slave traders (I mean labour collectors) and sugar planters. To the islanders themselves

> it has been in every way an unmitigated evil. In Queensland they work for fourpence a day, in Fiji for twopence: white labour for the same would cost at least five to eight shillings a day; the white man works eight hours a day, the poor Kanaka toils on from ten to fourteen, often dying from sheer exhaustion, and ending with the burial of a dog. In the slaving ships the immoralities are unspeakable.

Paton's statements are reinforced by evidence given before the Royal Commission which sat in Queensland in 1885.

At long last the Queensland Government abolished the Kanaka labour system at the end of 1890, but, as the Aborigines Protection Society pointed out at the time, 'there is danger of its being clandestinely continued in that colony, and also of its being encouraged in other parts in consequence of the humane change that has been appointed in Queensland.' These misgivings were quickly justified, for in 1892 Sir Samuel Griffith, Premier of Queensland, introduced a Bill allowing renewal of the traffic for a period of ten years. This was passed by the Colonial Legislature and assented to in the Queen's name by Sir Henry Norman, who believed the regulations framed for the prevention of abuses to be adequate. There is no doubt that under these regulations care was taken to protect the Polynesians in Queensland from such cruel treatment as was common in former years. But it does not appear that satisfactory arrangements were made to control either their recruitment in the islands or their return to their homes on the expiry of their service.

A debate on the subject took place in the House of Commons on May 26, 1892, in which Mr. A. J. Balfour said that 'they were all absolutely convinced of the evils that had attended this traffic in the past and that might attend it in the future,' and it was well pointed out by Mr. James Bryce (later Lord Bryce) that while there are grave difficulties in the way of any interference by the Imperial Government with the action of a colony endowed with so much independence as Queensland, it is competent for the home authorities—and clearly their duty—to see that no kidnapping or unjust recruiting is allowed in the Pacific Islands, which are 'outside the boundaries of Queensland and under the protection of the British flag.'

The Aborigines Protection Society held stoutly to the opinion that 'the system of Polynesian labour in Queensland has been proved—especially in the evidence laid before the Royal Commission of 1885—to be so injurious to native interests, and so entirely at variance with the recognised principles of English justice to inferior races, that no regulations for improving it can purge it of its essential evils.' A Blue Book published in 1895 [1] showed that Sir Henry Norman undoubtedly took the utmost pains to see that the traffic was carried on as humanely as possible and to punish persons convicted of ill-treating the labourers. But as Dr. Wilson, Bishop of Melanesia, temperately pointed out: 'Two wrongs are being committed against the islanders, which, unless removed, must bring discredit upon the sugar industry of Queensland. As now carried on, the trade does not lead to the civilisation but rather to the decivilisation of the islands. It leads also directly to their *depopulation*.' In 1898 the Aborigines Protection Society was able to report that 'the difficulties of obtaining fresh recruits from islands

[1] C. 7912.

already deprived of so many of their inhabitants, and the rigour with which regulations are enforced as regards both the recruiting and the treatment of the Polynesians while they are in Queensland, appear, however, to have rendered this form of slavery so costly and inconvenient that it is ceasing to be profitable. In this way there is a prospect of the pernicious and disgraceful traffic dying out.'

Thus was brought to an end, but to a not very creditable end, a traffic deeply discreditable to the British name in the Pacific. Much was due to the steady pressure of English reformers, but Parliament was hampered by the difficulty of interfering in the internal affairs of a colony to which, as some argued, self-governing powers had been too prematurely granted in 1859.

For fifty years a struggle has been waged, unhappily without much success, against abuses, closely akin to those of Kanaka labour, which have occurred in the New Hebrides. These islands have since 1906 been under the condominium of Great Britain and France, but the full story belongs to an earlier period. The recruiting of labour in the New Hebrides had been carried on in the past with the same abuses which had characterised the system in other parts of the Pacific. But the special feature in regard to the New Hebrides is the experiment of condominium, its inefficiency and its unfortunate results with regard to the treatment of the natives. Resolutions were passed by a Conference of the Protestant Churches held in the New Hebrides on June 24, 1913, 'calling the attention of the people of the British Empire to the deplorable condition of things existing in this group of Islands,' the gross inefficiency of the French National Court was pointed out, and the fact that most of the French judges knew no English, which meant that the evidence of natives had to undergo a double translation before it became intelligible to the majority of the Bench. The resolutions drew attention to the remission or failure to execute sentences upon French subjects, instancing a case of the kidnapping and murder of a native by a Frenchman who walked out of the court a free man. The British Courts, on the other hand, punished severely offences against natives. Other resolutions complained of the long imprisonment of natives awaiting their trial, and stated that 'whilst on British plantations fair conditions of life, work, and payment are generally maintained, the majority of French plantations furnish examples of an exploitation which can only be denominated slavery.'

In an article published on June 11, 1913, *Truth* stated that 'the scandal of the New Hebrides situation is that, while the regulations for the protection of the natives are strictly enforced against British "nationals," the French planters are permitted to break them with impunity.' A French periodical, *La France d'Outre Mer* (March, 1912), put the case with even greater frankness:

> the recruiting of native labour goes on in flagrant violation of the Convention of 1906 under abominable conditions. Slavery is, in fact, re-established. The natives are treated like beasts of burden . . . their work is overwhelming, their wages ridiculously small. . . . Alas! it has become nearly impossible to obtain voluntary labour, and so one of the most disgusting forms of slavery has been established in order to procure labourers. The settlers equip a boat and go from Island to Island; sometimes by craft and sometimes by violence they seize the native men and women whom they

want. This is what the English call 'kidnapping,' or as we call it in good French, 'la traite'—women and young girls are forcibly taken away from their husbands or relatives, and often find themselves at the mercy of the savage crews of the ships before they are sent to the plantations. Cases of sheer violence are numerous, and are established by irrefutable documents.

The existence of such gross abuses only twenty years ago may be startling to those who do not realise that Queensland, a self-governing British colony, had permitted or condoned similar abuses twenty years earlier, and that just as Britain had been fifteen years ahead of France in abolishing slavery, so there would probably be a similar time-lag before French standards of what constituted decent treatment for native labour reached the British level.

Reform in the New Hebrides is further complicated by the unworkable system of administration necessitated by that most unsatisfactory form of government, the condominium. The price the wretched natives have paid for that condominium can be gathered from the fact that it has been estimated that the population has been reduced from 600,000 in 1882 to 65,000 in 1911. Looking back over the Victorian era, one finds much that is depressing in the colonial attempts to substitute forms of disguised slavery for old systems which had become illegal.

But against the gloom must be set the fact that in the policy of the British Colonial Office the enlightened standards of colonial administration first laid down by Buxton and his Emancipators triumphed first in one area, then in another, in spite of occasional retrograde steps and more frequent displays of regrettable weakness in dealing with reactionary Colonial Governments and with the growing power of settler communities.

In West Africa progress was steady throughout the period. In New Zealand an enlightened policy for the Maoris was being evolved. In East Africa Lugard and Harry Johnstone were laying foundations of policy which, had they been continually applied, would have saved much national heartburning to-day. Towards the close of the Victorian era Abolitionists and Emancipators were looking hopefully to the consummation of their self-imposed tasks. Alas! how little they guessed that even at that time birth was given to new forms of slavery which would spell oppression, torture and bloodshed upon a scale, and of a character, as terrible as anything which had occurred a hundred years before.

CHAPTER X

The Servitude of Rubber and Cocoa—The Congo

The Inception of the Congo Free State—The 'Personal State'—Its Rubber and its Tragedy—The Brussels Conference—The Basis of the System—What 'Force' Meant—The Commission of Enquiry—Women Hostages—Destruction of both People and Rubber Vines—Flogging and Mutilation—The Public Conscience in Britain and Belgium—Emile Vandervelde—The Reformers—Reduction of Population—King Leopold's Profits—Belgian Annexation and the End of 'Congo Atrocities.'

'The contemplation of an immeasurable misery has caused us to publish this book.' [1]

Rev. Father Vermeersch, S.J.

'A monstrous anomaly—monstrous as much from the economic as from the human standpoint.'

Emile Vandervelde.

The story of the Congo Free State is full of grim paradoxes. Founded by King Leopold II of Belgium 'for the purpose of promoting the civilisation and commerce of Africa and for other human and benevolent purposes, it became the cruel and cold-blooded exploitation of people inhabiting a territory half as large as Europe.' At an early date its Sovereign declared that its 'only programme, I am anxious to repeat, is the work of moral and material regeneration.'

[1] A. Vermeersch, S.J., *La Question Congolaise*, 1906.

Yet if reliance can be placed upon published figures, the population in twenty-five years was reduced from at least 20,000,000 to about 8,000,000. One of the main reasons advanced for creating the Free State was to abolish Arab slavery, but it soon riveted on the necks of the unhappy negroes a slavery far more cruel, far more destructive of human life, than Arab slavery, and from which none could escape. This State, which undertook to give free and equal opportunities to the trade of all countries, developed into a rigid monopoly for the State and a few privileged and State-authorised concessionaires.

Even now the world has not fully realised the disastrous nature of the Congo experiment in colonial administration. But its horrors stand for all governments as such a warning against confusing the functions of commerce and administration, that it may be hoped the world will never again witness such an attempt to exploit the weaker races for the sake of profit.

The Congo experiment is now seen to have been not only one of the cruellest crimes, but one of the most colossal mistakes in the history of the world. Religious persecutions have had behind them the sanctions of religion. International wars have based justification on the plea of national defence or national expansion. The Congo crime had no extenuating circumstances, no palliative and no excuse. It was just a sordid exploitation of human beings for personal gain.

The Belgian Government and people were at no time responsible for the creation of the Congo Free State, nor for its system of exploitation. Individual Belgians shared in the colossal profits made out of rubber, individual Belgians served under King Leopold's

Congo Administration, but so did Italian, Scandinavian, American and even British subjects. The founding of the Congo Free State, the development of its system of exploitation, the crudeness of its administration, the demoralisation and suffering of its population, were as King Leopold himself declared, his personal creation—'the result of my labour.'

The Congo Free State (to-day Belgian Congo) is a vast equatorial territory, covering over 900,000 square miles. King Leopold's wide imagination had for years played with the idea of developing this great region. Stanley's famous expedition in 1874 to 1877, through the Dark Continent, gave the King the information which he had long sought regarding the native population, the course of the Congo River, and the natural resources of the country. When Stanley, on his return, landed at Marseilles in January, 1878, he was met on behalf of the King by General Sanford (Secretary of the International African Association, already formed by the King). Stanley was told that 'his discoveries had given birth to a grand project, for the realisation of which his experience and active assistance were needed.' In the succeeding years Stanley, acting as Agent for the future Congo State already conceived by the King, was employed to negotiate treaties with a large number of native chiefs, and, in general, to open up the Congo Basin. Stanley himself described his task as

> the novel mission of sowing along its banks civilised settlements to peacefully conquer and subdue it, to remould it in harmony with modern ideas into National States, within whose limits the European merchant shall go hand in hand with the dark African trader, and justice, law and order shall

prevail and murder and lawlessness and the cruel barter of slaves shall for ever cease.[1]

The realisation of King Leopold's African ambitions was impossible without international recognition, and to obtain this his endeavours were directed for several years. Those who had inherited the emancipation fervour of Wilberforce and Buxton were sought out and their support solicited for what appeared to be a great and noble ideal. They were given the most explicit assurances by the King of his good intentions towards the natives. They were even royally entertained in Brussels—but some doubted!

Finally, as the result of the Berlin Conference of Fourteen Powers, held during 1884 and 1885, the Congo Free State was created for the regeneration of Africa and the development of trade, and received the tacit approval of the civilised world. The new-born State was placed under the personal sovereignty of King Leopold, not unconditionally, but under certain definite conditions laid down in the Berlin Act: these included complete freedom of trade, the open door, no monopolies, and the fullest consideration for the protection and welfare of the natives. 'All the Powers exercising sovereign rights or influence in the aforesaid territories bind themselves to watch over the preservation of the native tribes—to care for the improvement of the conditions of their moral and material well-being.' They bound themselves also 'to help in suppressing slavery and especially the slave trade.'

[1] It is one amongst the many Congo tragedies that Stanley should have lived long enough to see the 'philanthropic State,' which he had helped to create, grow up into a monster of oppression.

In 1889 and 1890 a second Conference was held, this time at Brussels, which reaffirmed the benevolent intentions of the Powers towards the natives, and gave King Leopold what he wanted from the Powers, permission to impose limited import duties for the ostensible purpose of putting down the Arab slave trade. But it did one thing more, it provided King Leopold with the means to create and arm a native force, and on the other hand gave him the power to disarm the people of the Congo, who were thus rendered defenceless and helpless for the first stage of the Congo system of exploitation. In the course of a few years the Arab power was indeed, after heavy fighting, completely broken. But the enslavement of the whole population took the place of the local and incidental Arab slavery, whilst the limited import duties grew into a prohibition of all trade except by the State and a few favoured concessionaire companies.

In the early years after the creation of the Congo Free State the conditions laid down by the Berlin Act were not grossly infringed. The earlier arrivals in the Congo traded honestly and without more than comparatively isolated incidents of cruelty and oppression.

But in 1889 the cloven hoof began to show itself in ordinances which took from the natives their hitherto undisputed right to collect or trade in ivory and rubber, gum-copal, wax and other natural products from the recesses of their own forests.

The years 1890–93 saw the commencement, and before long the establishment, of the principle that the natives had no right to the land (outside their own gardens and villages) nor to its products. These years saw also the virtual ending of the freedom of trade promised by the Berlin Act to all countries, and the beginnings of forced labour in the 'prestations' (forced levies) introduced by Captain Dhanis, who became later Baron Dhanis, Governor-General of the State.

If man invented motor cars for our comfort, then the devil inspired the machinery for squeezing rubber out of the miserable Congo natives. If the opening up of the Congo had not coincided with the vastly increased European demand for rubber, resulting from the development of motor cars and bicycles, it is possible that the history of the Congo Free State would not be one of which Europe must for ever be ashamed. But with increasing demand came soaring prices. Rubber to-day stands at less than 4*d.* per lb. In 1897 Congo rubber sold at 3*s.* 7*d.*, in 1910 at 8*s.* 7*d.* (with plantation rubber at 12*s.* 5*d.*). The temptation was too great. 'Haste, haste, get what rubber you can,' was the frantic urge from Brussels. The result was not merely colossal loss of human life, but widespread destruction of the wild rubber vines of the forest.

By about the year 1897 the 'system' was nearly full grown. It is necessary that the fundamental principles of that system should be well understood, in order that the colossal cruelty to which it gave rise should not be regarded merely as 'regrettable incidents.' The basis of the Congo system was that all the wealth in the country, all the means of distribution, control and marketing belonged to the State.

If this appears to resemble the doctrines of nineteenth-century Socialism, the fact must not be overlooked that it was being applied in an uncivilised land under an absolutism which could truly say '*L'Etat c'est moi.*' And that the only interest of this unique State was the extraction of wealth. The natives had no voice, and at that time no defenders, and their social and economic life were alike blasted.

From time immemorial 'the keen, enterprising, high-spirited peoples' (as Stanley described them) had shown vigour, enterprise and marked aptitude for trading. Yet it was decreed that they possessed nothing, and that everything belonged to the State. Their position was summed up in a remarkable phrase used by M. Smet de Nayer, Prime Minister of Belgium: 'The native is entitled to nothing. What is given to him is a mere gratuity.' Another speaker remarked of that phrase: 'A man has been found to make of that phrase "the native is entitled to nothing"—a system!'

The 'system' struck at the roots of native social life, it robbed the people of all initiative and enterprise and condemned them to the position of hewers of wood and drawers of water, 'entitled to nothing.' Having robbed them of all incentive to gather the natural wealth of the country, the Congo administration was compelled to substitute the only alternative to commerce, namely, force.

What did force spell?

The answer to this question is to be found in a mass of reports from consular officers and merchants of all nations, missionaries of all denominations, commercial agents, travellers, naval and military officers. Their evidence would fill many volumes, but for the purpose of this book only the most authoritative and unchallengeable is reproduced, principally that of the Commission of Enquiry, which an outraged public opinion compelled the Sovereign of the Congo Free State to send out in 1904–5, a Commission composed of three judges, Belgian, Swiss and Italian. This Commission reported to the King, and upon him alone rested responsibility for publication.

During the enquiry Foreign Secretaries of other countries had been officially assured that the evidence would be published. Men on the spot who were daily witnesses of the atrocities were convinced that the ghastly nature of the evidence would so horrify the civilised world that the King would never dare to publish it. They said so publicly, and the men on the spot proved right. King Leopold would only allow, and that after a year's delay and conflict with the President of the Commission, the issue of the General Report. Critics who tendered the evidence have always maintained that this royal suppression of their evidence taken on the spot is in itself a sufficient confirmation of the truth of their testimony.

But the Report, restrained though it was, proved up to the hilt the truth of all the horrible evidence which missionaries, consuls, merchants and others had given to the world during the years 1892–1904, and rendered supremely ridiculous the efforts made by the King's friends to dismiss all this evidence as the vapourings of 'worthy souls whose reserves of sentimentalism are often injudiciously employed.' (Speech in the Belgian Chamber by M. Carton de Wiart.)

The system, as we have seen, was based upon the appropriation of all the natural wealth of the land. In order to induce the natives to collect it for 'nothing' (*vide* M. de Smet de Nayer), force was inevitable. The machinery of force was crudely simple. At Boma, the capital, dwelt the Governor-General. Under him, scattered over the country, were some 2,000 white agents, each in control of a given number of villages, under whose command were native soldiers, recruited mainly from the most savage tribes of the interior, often cannibals. They alone were armed with rifles, for all importation of firearms for the use of the natives had been prohibited by the Treaty of Berlin.

But how in practice was this force to be used to collect the rubber? The density of the forest made it impracticable to put a gun behind every collector of rubber, or to commandeer the men of the villages and send them in gangs to gather rubber, as in the plantation system. What better plan—or indeed what other plan was possible—than to drive the men folk to gather rubber (or copal, as the case might be) by making hostages of their wives and children? This, in the main, was the plan adopted. In practice—true, it was a devilish invention—it worked! A village was ordered to provide, say, 50 or 100 baskets of rubber a week. If it failed to produce the full amount, native soldiers, or 'sentinels,' as they were sometimes called in the territories of the concessionaire companies —were sent armed with rifles into the villages to capture the women, children and very old men. The veriest tyro in colonial affairs can depict the result—the feeble defence of the unarmed husbands and sons, the rape of women, the cries of little children, the burning and pillage of the huts, the unnameable atrocities. As the native proverb had it: 'Rubber is death.'

The white agents, who included not Belgians alone, but the failures of other nationalities also, were often, indeed, to be pitied, for they arrived in debt for passage and outfit, and could not break away from the machine that had caught them in its wheels. A few committed suicide, overwhelmed by the loneliness, climate and the inevitable and appalling cruelty of the system which they were forced to administer. The greater number accepted the system with seared consciences, and at the day of judgment some will have to answer for atrocities almost beyond belief. They were wretchedly paid, but the famous Bonus Proclamation issued from Brussels on June 20, 1892, permitted and indeed invited them to increase their earnings by a diabolically calculated system of bonuses. Thus for every kilo of rubber or copal screwed out of the natives at a cost of 5 centimes or less, the agent received a bonus of 15 centimes. But if through laxity or sense of justice he paid the native 6 or 7 centimes a kilo, his bonus was reduced to 10 centimes, and so on. Thus was a premium placed on criminal extortion.

The actual executive instruments of extortion in the Congo of the Sovereign will in Brussels were the soldiers of the 'Force Publique' or the 'Sentinels,' who were billeted upon the villages, and of whom the Commission reported to King Leopold: 'Of how many abuses [atrocities] the native sentinels have been guilty, it would be impossible to say.' And in another passage: 'they kill without pity.' But the ultimate responsibility for unimaginable cruelties rests not with these savages, liable to be flogged themselves if the supply of rubber was short, not altogether with the degraded white agents ordered at all costs to increase the supply of rubber and broken if they failed,[1] not even with the Governor-General at Boma, who was there with definite orders, but with the system which existed for the purpose of making vast profits for the royal shareholder and his creatures in Brussels. The natives fled from their villages in thousands. Refugees, trying to escape from this 'Free State' in which liberty could only be found in death, told the British Consul that they were 'going where there is no rubber.' Rubber was literally death to large numbers of the unhappy collectors. A British Consul writes that 'of every 50 sent into the forest to gather rubber not more than 25 or 30 returned. The rest had fallen from trees or died of disease, hardship, hunger or the attacks of wild beasts.'

As the rubber vines became exhausted, the unfortunate native had to go many miles into the forest to find it. King Leopold's Commission of Enquiry stated that:

> When once he (the native) has collected the rubber he must bring it to the State station or to that of the Company and only then can he return to his village, where he can sojourn for barely more than 2 or 3 days, because the next demand is upon him.

Meanwhile their wives were left in the villages at the mercy of the agent and the native soldiers, whom it was one of their tasks to feed. Each woman had

[1] Speak as follows to the owner thereof: 'Go to the forest at once and if in a week you have not returned with 10 lbs. of rubber, I shall set fire to your hut and you will burn.'—Extract from Official Order.

'Everywhere on the Congo the native only collects rubber under the influence of force.'—Report of Commission.

to furnish every 4, 8 or 10 days a given quantity of Kwanga or native bread. The Commissioners remark:

> There is an unanimous testimony to the heavy burden imposed on the women in some villages by the incessancy of the demand. . . . The most painful side of the task is its continuity. As chikanwe (another name for native bread) keeps badly, the task is never done and haunts the woman continually, making her life a perfect drudgery.

A subsidiary principle of the Congo exploitation was that 'the administration must live on the country'!

Making and supplying bread was not the only drudgery. There were other imposts of food. Fish, fresh from lake or river, had to be supplied in very large quantities. The Commission noted that

> the quantity demanded is often out of proportion to the diminished population on which it is imposed . . . People . . . are compelled to convey their fish (dried) every fortnight, by canoe, 70 or 80 kilometres to New Antwerp, and have often suffered imprisonment when behindhand through no fault of their own.

There were also

> impositions in fresh food destined exclusively for the white man. The Commission has witnessed for itself the growing scarcity and consequent dearness of sheep, goats, fowls and ducks, and accounts for it by the fact that instead of being an object of trade, they are demanded as an impost, sometimes without adequate payment.

The Commission pointed out that 'Apart from the taxes on victuals, the natives are required to furnish to the State a certain amount of labour: wood-cutting, work at stations, canoeing and portage,' and that 'The 80 steamers that sail on the waters of the Congo and its affluents are dependent upon a supply of wood for fuel.' The Commissioners' restrained comment is that 'this tax is sometimes excessive.'

The demand for porters was yet another exaction. The Commissioners state that: 'The quantity of goods transported is enormous, while the population is scanty, and, as a consequence, the same individuals are regularly charged with the labour. Moreover, provisions are rare, and almost always unequal to the victualling of the caravans of carriers. Magistrates have testified to the sad consequences of porterage, which crushes the unhappy populations subjected to it and threatens them with partial destruction.' Or, as Sir Charles Dilke expressed it in Parliament with greater vividness but perfect accuracy: 'These miserable savages were used and allowed to die in the same way in which some inhuman companies worked their omnibus horses, simply working them till they died, because it was cheaper.'

The Commissioners reserve what is perhaps their most severe condemnation for the system of black overseers in the villages: 'According to the witnesses, they abuse their authority and become despots, demanding women and victuals, not only for themselves, but for the following of vagabond parasites whom the love of rapine attaches to them like a regular bodyguard. They kill without pity all who offer resistance to their demands or caprices. . . .' And again, in the Lulonga district, 'the capitas or black overseers are veritable despots. The abuses of the system are so grave that the Commissioners are forced to the conclusion that it ought to be suppressed wherever possible.'

The British Consul, Mr. Nightingale, who knew the

Congo as few men did, said that the natives were worked '304 days a year for 6*s*. 4*d*. If the quantities [of food or rubber] are deficient, the penalties are whipping or imprisonment. The natives are unanimously of opinion that they were better off under the Arabs.' The penalties for failure to comply with any of these ceaseless and exorbitant demands recall the Conquest of Mexico in their almost incredible cruelty. The excesses of cannibalism, mutilations, tortures and unnameable atrocities reported by missionaries, merchants and native chiefs have never been refuted; moreover, if they were not carried out by direct orders they were frequently committed with the knowledge of and sometimes the actual participation of the white agents. The punishments formally approved by the Administration were those of the slaver; punishments not for crime, but for failure to provide sufficient rubber, food or labour. Flogging with the chicotte was an everyday occurrence. It is thus described by an experienced English traveller who had witnessed it only too often:

'The chicotte of raw hippo hide, trimmed like a corkscrew, with edges like knife-blades, is a terrible instrument, and a few blows bring blood. . . . It needs an extraordinary constitution to withstand the terrible punishment of 100 blows.'

He goes on to say:

> It is bad enough the flogging of men, but far worse is the punishment inflicted on women and children. Small boys of ten or twelve, with excitable hot-tempered masters, are often most harshly treated. . . . Five women who had deserted were in chains at Riba-Riba; all were cut very badly, having been most severely chicotted or flogged.

The Commission noted that on the Lulonga 'the whip was habitually employed,' and the flogging of 'collectors who have not furnished their full impositions' was usual.

Probably the maximum amount of suffering was caused by the hostage system, to which reference has already been made. To put the women and girls in the hostage house, working them in the chain gang by day, was an effective method of bringing pressure to bear upon their husbands and fathers.

These hostage houses (Maisons d'otage) were veritable charnel houses, usually constructed of 'wattle and daub' walls with grass roof. They were without ventilation or sanitary arrangements and their capacity of say thirty persons was choked with three times its number. All ages of both sexes were crowded into them—children were conceived and children were born in them side by side with the dying, for when the door was opened in the morning one of the first tasks was usually that of bringing out the dead. Appeals to separate the sexes were met with ribald refusals.

There is no doubt that the 'system' brutalised every human agency connected with the supreme objective of producing rubber. The judiciary itself was contaminated. How otherwise can the following statement in the Commissioners' Report be explained?

'Distinguished magistrates, who have been most helpful to the Commission in their search for the truth, have affirmed that, in their opinion, the retention of women as hostages is the gentlest, most humane and most efficacious means of coercion.'

The assertion that this was the 'most humane' method throws lurid light on the less humane methods.

That it was efficacious none would deny, but what can be said of the mentality that devised a system of rubber production based upon hitting men through their wives and daughters?

When it is realised that the savage soldiery had the women hostages at their mercy at all times of day or night the anxiety of their husbands, far away in the forests collecting rubber, can be understood. A missionary, the Rev. Somerville Gilchrist, wrote:

> I shall never forget the impression left on my mind by one of these horrible Houses of Detention. It was a small, low-roofed circular building, with the only entrance to it through another building of the same type. The latter was occupied by a number of sentries with Albini rifles. Inside the other were herded a large number of women, girls and boys—a mass of bones held together by black skin. I addressed myself to one poor skeleton of a woman lying in front of me where I stood. I asked her if she was sick. 'Two days ago,' she answered, 'I gave birth to a child and oh, white man, I am dying of hunger. I've had nothing to eat.' She was so weak that it was with difficulty she could articulate her words—And oh, the faces of those others! The horror of it! Outside the building there was a row of those skeleton women on the chain, followed by a sentry with an Albini and a chicotte, going back and forward from the garden to the river.

That rape, murder and outrage were common is not surprising in view of the barbarous and savage human agents who were employed.

The destruction of the authority of the chiefs was another part of the deliberate policy of the Administration. Heartrending passages in the evidence given by missionaries describe how the chiefs came to them, utterly broken in body and mind. One of the more important chiefs, whose evidence is quoted by the Commission, brought 120 twigs, each representing a murder in his village by sentinels. He told King Leopold's Commission how his beard of many years' growth had been chopped off, how he had been chicotted, imprisoned, and put to the most menial labour by the agent of the Concession. The mutilated wife of another chief showed her footless leg and hernia, the price she had paid for being faithful to her husband, who, protesting, was cruelly flogged.

Irrespective of the abominable cruelty to the chiefs, the gross impolicy of undermining the age-long native foundations of law and order without attempting to supply any just or effective substitute is one more proof that the Congo Free State was not in any true sense of the word a Government, but a vampire which preyed upon human life and upon the natural wealth of the country whilst giving nothing in return.

The Commission merely confirmed all that missionaries and other independent witnesses had been saying for years when they stated, in referring to one of the Concessions, that 'the imprisonment of female hostages, the subjection of chiefs to servile labour, the humiliations inflicted on them, the flogging of india-rubber hands and brutalities by black prison guards were habitually practised.'

The Commission referred sternly to the punitive expeditions against villages :

> It is not astonishing that sometimes the most murderous consequences have followed. The expedition may easily degenerate into massacre, accompanied by fire and pillage, the punishment being in flagrant disproportion to the fault and the innocent suffering with the guilty.

Guilty of what ? Guilt connotes crime, and the only crime of the simple Congo natives was the defence of their women; their only offence, if offence it be, inability to gather enough rubber to satisfy the rapacity of their white overlords. They had no legal means of redress. Many districts as large as Belgium had never seen or even heard of a magistrate, who might be a thousand miles away. He, in turn, was dependent for his very bread upon the local agent or concessionaire. The Commissioners advised

> that it is the moral enfranchisement of the magistrate from his dependence upon the administrative authority that is most urgent.

This was indeed very diplomatic phrasing!

The Commissioners write very frankly with regard to the hardships suffered by native witnesses required to give evidence at Boma, the capital, nearly three weeks' journey from most of the rubber areas:

> All the magistrates testify that a large number of black witnesses forced to travel from the Haut Congo to Boma, never see their village again, but die on the journey . . . the mortality is increased by the fact that on their journey and at their destination they are often badly lodged and insufficiently fed. The very name of 'Boma' frightens the native. . . . The inhabitant of the Upper Congo, cited as a witness, flees to the forest or the bush. He must be treated as a prisoner, hunted, perhaps chained, or at any rate, constraint must be used.

The Report paid a remarkable tribute to the Evangelical missionaries: 'They acquire ascendancy, not only over the natives subjected to their religious teaching, but over all the villages whose griefs they hear. The missionary becomes, for the native of a district, the sole representative of equity and justice. He adds to the ascendancy acquired by his religious zeal the prestige which, in the interests of the State, should belong to the magistrate' (of whom there were none in most missionary regions !).

The result of twenty-five years of misrule was depopulation such as might have been caused by the ravages of the Black Death. The grand aggregate of destruction—a native population of between 20 and 30 millions reduced to about 8 millions, was given at the beginning of this chapter. As early as 1899, after only seven years of the 'system,' Mr. Grogan, an experienced English traveller, wrote that 'A country apparently well populated, and responsive to just treatment in Lugard's time, is now practically a howling wilderness: the scattered inhabitants, living almost without cultivation in the marshes, thickets and reeds, madly fleeing even from their own shadows.'

The Commissioners themselves state that 'it is certain that a great proportion of the population must have disappeared. . . . Where the impositions, unevenly divided, weigh too heavily, . . . anxiety and consequent depression have resulted in depopulation . . . on the least alarm they (the natives) fled to the bush and the islands of the river, whence a considerable mortality has resulted.'

Sir H. M. Stanley estimated that the population of the Congo at the founding of the Free State was about 40,000,000. It is probable that Stanley over-estimated its density. But if Stanley's estimate is halved and the figure taken at 20,000,000, which would be the density of neighbouring territories, the admitted decrease in the population would be 12,000,000 !

The following figures of decline in population were given by the British Consul in the Lukoléla district: a population of 5,000 in 1887 was reduced in 1903 to

600. Near Lake Tumba, fourteen villages with 12,320 inhabitants in 1893 had only 1,610 inhabitants in 1903. Three towns with a population estimated formerly at between 4,000 and 5,000 had disappeared altogether. The villages that remained were overgrown with weeds. The 'serfs,' as Father Vermeersch called them, had no time to cultivate their gardens.

The system was as wasteful of the fruits of nature as of the lives of men. Was it cynicism that caused King Leopold to write: 'Our refined society attaches to human life, and with reason, a value unknown to barbarous communities'? His attitude and that of his officials to the native was expressed in the oft-repeated dictum that the native 'only respects the law of force, knows no other persuasion than terror.'[1] The Prime Minister, M. de Smet de Nayer, asked rhetorically in the Belgian Chamber: 'Can civilisation be founded without, as its basis, the Christian law of work?' And when Emile Vandervelde, the courageous opponent of the Congo System, interjected: 'Leave Christianity out of this business!' M. de Smet de Nayer asked him 'Would you allow the negro to wallow in idleness and sloth?' forgetting that in seven years these 'idle' natives had produced £11,000,000 worth of rubber from their own forests for the King and his associates!

The ghastly truth took long to penetrate the public conscience. The Congo was remote and the civilised world had accepted at its face value King Leopold's declaration regarding the 'humane and beneficent purposes' for which the Congo Free State had been founded. Although a handful of British and American

[1] President of the Appeal Court of the Lower Congo.

missionaries had for some years been protesting vainly to the Congo authorities regarding the abominable treatment of the natives, for Europe the veil was first lifted by the publication (after his death in 1895) of the Diary of Stanley's young lieutenant, E. J. Glave.

At a meeting in London in 1897, called by the Aborigines Protection Society, whose Secretary, Mr. H. R. Fox-Bourne, had commenced at an earlier date to expose the Congo crime, a Swedish missionary, the Rev. E. V. Sjöblom, lately returned in broken health, described the mutilations and all the other horrors of the system. He had himself been threatened by the Governor-General, Baron Wahis, with five years' penal servitude for daring to protest. In 1899 a Frenchman, Baron de Mandat Grance, who with M. Pierre Mille had visited the Congo, wrote that 'the race which has survived three centuries of the slave trade will be destroyed by fifty years of philanthropy.'

Truth was on the march. In this country the spiritual forces which Wilberforce and Buxton had created still lived and it was not long before they became convinced that, in the words of Archbishop Davidson, 'Negro slavery had been resuscitated in perhaps its darkest and reddest form in the Congo.' In due course many of the actual descendants and relatives of Buxton, Wilberforce, Hodgkin, Sturge and Fox were busily engaged in rousing public opinion in protest against a more extensive and atrocious system of slavery than that which their forefathers had fought so tenaciously.

The Free Churches responded to the cry of slavery with all their old ardour, the more fervently that from their ranks came most of the Congo missionaries.

The Congo Reform Association was formed with E. D. Morel, a doughty fighter, as its very able Secretary. Large numbers of public meetings were held and addressed by lately returned missionaries, by bishops, clergy, social reformers, political leaders, African travellers and colonial administrators.

The responsibility of Great Britain, as one of the signatories to the Berlin Act, was urged upon the Government by the reformers in Parliament. No less than fourteen debates took place, in which Sir Charles Dilke, Mr. (later Sir) Herbert Samuel, Mr. Alfred (later Lord) Emmott, and Mr. (later Sir) Ernest Bennett took leading parts. This country had no axe of her own to grind. First and foremost she wanted to secure decent treatment for the natives, as guaranteed by the Berlin Act.

Lord Lansdowne, who was at the Foreign Office during the earlier years, summarised Congo misrule as 'bondage under the most barbarous and inhuman conditions, and maintained for mercenary motives of the most selfish character.' Sir Edward Grey, speaking also as Foreign Secretary, said in 1904 that 'Our position as an Imperial Power in Africa made us unable to tolerate with safety a vampire slave state on our immediate borders.' At a later period, not long before the Congo Free State was annexed by the Belgian Government, he trusted that the change would produce, 'not a list of reforms, but an entire change of the system.' Throughout the British campaign for reform, he combined moderation of language with a patience which to the reformers appeared at times excessive. Speaking in 1908, a few months before Belgian annexation took place, Mr. Ramsay MacDonald (then Chairman of the Parliamentary Committee of the Congo Reform Association) said: 'Patience is a virtue up to a point. It then becomes one of the most abominable vices with which humanity is afflicted.' Lord Cromer's condemnation was crushing; speaking in the House of Lords, in March, 1908, he declared that 'never in my experience have I seen or heard of misrule comparable to the abuses that have grown up in the Congo State.'

In this country the demand for reform was powerful, but the position in Belgium was very different and the heroic Belgian reformers are well worthy of a place beside Wilberforce and Buxton. First in honour come Emile Vandervelde, leader of the Socialist Party; Georges Lorand, the Liberal leader; Father Vermeersch, of the Society of Jesus; and Professor Cattier, of the University of Brussels. This handful had to face the unscrupulous opposition of King Leopold, supremely powerful, able and rich, supported by ministers entirely obedient to his wishes and policy and by a Parliament most of whose members were either subservient or indifferent.

The Belgian people, with whom one has great sympathy, were without colonial experience or tradition, and took no real interest in the Congo, and when the prospect of annexing that unhappy and misgoverned country was forced upon their attention, were not unreasonably apprehensive that the cost of reform would come out of their pockets, as, indeed, it did.

The Belgian Press, with two honourable exceptions, was subserviently pro-Congo, and to a large extent in the pay of the King. The leaders of the Church had been inspired by Cardinal Lavigerie in 1889 to support the Congo Free State as a Christian undertaking which was to stamp out Arab slavery. The Catholic missions on the spot were in a dependent position and it was difficult for them to speak out, but some, like Father Vermeersch, played a noble part. His book on the Congo atrocities came, in his own words, from 'the contemplation of an immeasurable misery,' and he declared boldly that 'the rubber belongs to the natives' and that they were 'the slaves or serfs of the public authority.' The Jesuits, to their everlasting honour, repudiated grants of land made to them by the Congo administration. 'No one can compel us to co-operate in an injustice,' wrote Father Cas to the King's Minister, M. de Cuvelier.

When the Report of the Commission of Enquiry was allowed, at last, to be made public in October, 1905, opinion in Belgium began to change. Professor Cattier followed up an earlier exposure of the Congo Free State with his 'Etude sur la situation de l'Etat Independant du Congo,' in which he revealed not only its gross maladministration and oppression, but also the interesting fact that its Sovereign and his associates had made personal profits of £3,000,000 during the ten years 1896 to 1905, although the published accounts of the State had been so manipulated as to show a loss of £1,085,519.

Gradually the truth gained strength, but King Leopold continued to defy public opinion, and in writing to the three principal secretaries of the Congo State in June, 1906, he proclaimed majestically his own personal responsibility: 'My rights on the Congo are indivisible, they are the result of my toil. . . . No one was called upon to participate in my efforts. The Congo has thus been and can only have been a personal work.' He said that the Congo State had put an end to the slave trade and must now concentrate upon conquering sleeping-sickness. 'If God gives me that satisfaction I shall be able to present myself before His tribunal with the credit of having performed one of the finest acts of the century, and a legion of rescued beings will call down upon me his grace.'

The main battleground was by force of circumstances in the Belgian Chamber, and in debate after debate Vandervelde and Lorand fought against heavy odds for the oppressed natives of the Congo. Vandervelde saw clearly that, as he wrote in March, 1907, 'The King's policy is to delay as much as possible the time when Congolese absolutism will have to give way before Belgian constitutionalism.' Vandervelde realised that it would be impossible to combine reform with a balanced budget, at least until the exhausted country had recovered, but he believed it to be Belgium's duty to foot the bill. Early in 1908 he went himself to the Congo, his last utterance before setting out being a noble appeal to the Chamber to 'have pity upon the Congo natives.'

Annexation took place in August, 1908, but the King's ministers continued to fight a rearguard action in defence of forced labour, which M. Renkin, Minister of Justice, declared to be 'necessary, or civilisation is arrested.'

In April, 1909, the heir to the Belgian throne, now King Albert, took a courageous course and set sail for the Congo to see for himself. What he reported on his return has never been published, but it can be safely assumed that it was a powerful aid in the task of reforming the Administration.

Even after annexation reform was slow in coming, for as Mr. Ramsay MacDonald said in the House of Commons in February, 1909, 'the Belgian Government had taken over practically *en bloc* the old laws, practically the whole of the objectionable officials of the Congo Free State, introduced a Congo budget based on slave labour and adopted a system of forced labour on public works.'

The more extreme cruelties were checked, but not abolished, and still continued in the Concession areas, while the great problems of the natives' rights to the products and ownership of the land and to the free disposal of their labour cannot be said to have reached a satisfactory solution even to-day.

Meanwhile King Leopold's attitude of majestic and unshaken defiance remained unabated. At the great colonial festivities held at Antwerp in June, 1909, he said: 'The greatest satisfaction of my life has been to give the Congo to Belgium. The Congo is richer than you think. The duty of a sovereign is to enrich the nation.'

How different this language of 1909 from that at the founding of the Congo Free State. Then, his 'only programme, I am anxious to repeat, is the moral and material regeneration of the natives'; now, it had become the sordid objective of the enrichment of the European speculator!

During twenty years he had inoculated the Belgian mind with the poisonous idea that a tropical dependency exists for the sole purpose of enriching metropolitan interests. But he left to Belgium a legacy of debt, a country with its natural resources squandered, its population reduced, broken and embittered. Belgium entered indeed upon a *damnosa heritas* and it may be that the Government delayed first annexation, and then reform, because they realised that to clean out the Augean stable would be an almost superhuman task so long as the King remained to obstruct. Speaking in London in May, 1911, not long after the King's death, M. Vandervelde was able to say :

> This work of emancipation is now going well ahead. Leopold II is dead and, sad to say, his death in itself sufficed, even before all the reforms had been accomplished, to lighten the miserable lot of the unhappy natives. Belgium has assumed responsibility for the administration of the Congo. . . . Reforms have been decreed which are tending to the establishment therein of a normal rule. But for us, nothing will have been done while there remains something to be accomplished. The great Concessions are not yet abolished. Forced labour persists with, it is true, modifications, in one half of Congo. . . . Nevertheless, the most difficult task is done.

M. Vandervelde has never relaxed his noble efforts on behalf of the Congo natives. He has continued to watch over their interests, and only last summer initiated a debate in the Belgian Chamber on the question of forced labour. Recent reports made to the Slavery Committee of the League of Nations by the Belgian Government acknowledge the persistence of slavery in some parts of the Congo and of forced labour for food production and other purposes.

Owing to her limited experience as a Colonial Power, Belgium has still too few men possessing the necessary knowledge and tradition. But it is one of time's most welcome revenges that a distinguished Belgian, Dr.

Gohr, the value of whose work in abolishing slavery is universally acknowledged, has been twice Chairman of the Slavery Commission of the League of Nations.

Lord Cromer pointed out one of the principal lessons to be learned from the unhappy past of the Congo Free State when he said that 'Any attempt to combine in the same hands the powers of administration and commercial exploitation can only result in maladministration on the one hand and in commercial disappointment on the other.' In the world to-day there are still territories where the exploitation of the weaker races is in direct conflict with the League principle of Trusteeship.

The Congo Free State will be to all generations a hideous object lesson. It is to be hoped that history will never repeat itself and that it will remain unique—or in M. Vandervelde's words: 'A monstrous anomaly.'

CHAPTER XI

THE SERVITUDE OF RUBBER AND COCOA— PUTUMAYO RUBBER

Hardenburg's Story—The British Select Committee—The Putumayo System—Action by Sir Edward Grey—Mr. Justice Swinfen Eady on Company's Records—The Atrocities—Swinfen Eady orders Company to be wound up—The Opponents—Mr. Charles Roberts.

DURING the last years of the nineteenth century a familiar figure in the streets of Iquitos was a bare-footed hawker peddling cheap panama straws. In December, 1908, in the City of London, there was founded a company called the Peruvian Amazon Rubber Company, with a capital of one million sterling, and at its head was the erstwhile pedlar, now Julio Cesar Arana. The company surrounding him was of mixed nationality, and included several well-known British financiers.

In the midsummer of 1909 there came to London an unknown young man who had spent some years of his life in America as a civil engineer, W. E. Hardenburg, carrying with him a manuscript which contained his experiences in the Putumayo and its tributary rivers. This manuscript and the documents accompanying it were closely scrutinised by certain publishing houses, and these all with one accord refused to risk a publication unless adequately guaranteed against the consequences of legal proceedings. But the Editor of *Truth* and certain other British papers published considerable extracts.

The tragic story told by Mr. Hardenburg concerned the Indians of the Putumayo, of whom it was estimated there were about 60,000 : 'a simple people of naturally friendly disposition, whose confidence and affection it would not be difficult to gain.' In the basin of the Putumayo the forests contained considerable quantities of raw india-rubber fetching at that time 3*s.* per lb. in the markets of London and Antwerp. These Indians were enslaved by the Peruvian Amazon Company for the purpose of gathering this rubber from forests under a system which bore a close resemblance to that of King Leopold in the Congo. Dr. Paredes, of Iquitos, a writer of some note, issued at this time his book describing the results of the system :

> Their insatiable desire to obtain the greatest production in the least time and with the least possible expense was undoubtedly one of the causes of crime, for the Indians who did not comply with the requirements imposed were tortured and killed outright, while the stubborn ones were compelled with machete and bullet to fulfil the mandates. Crime was in proportion to the yield and the former [*sic*] increased, the greater was the number of kilograms extracted : that is, the greater the number of assassinations, the greater the production, which meant that a great part of the production was obtained over blood and dead bodies.

The system of rubber slavery revealed in the Putumayo challenged British sentiment, and challenged it successfully. Once again a handful of reformers succeeded in shattering an organisation powerfully entrenched in the City of London, and supported by a few persons occupying high positions in the social scale. A very real tragedy in this case, as in all other cases of slavery, was the time taken to carry the three essential stages; first, that of gathering authenticated facts; secondly, the rousing of public opinion; and thirdly, that of persuading Governments to take action. Fowell Buxton's letters and diaries show how heavily delay and its consequences lay upon his conscience during his sixteen years' task of securing the emancipation of slaves in British territories. A Select Committee of the House of Commons commented upon this important and cruel factor of delay in its valuable report upon the Putumayo:

> The delay during these months is greatly to be deplored. It is not merely a speculative question as to the light it throws on the minds of the British directors. But while they wrote leisurely debating replies to the Foreign Office the killing and torture of the helpless Indians was in fact going on all the time, and some of the worst atrocities were being perpetrated. They continued, in fact, till the break-up of the criminal gang of employees as the result of the discovery of the truth.

It is probably true to say that the cruelties committed upon the 60,000 Indians of the Putumayo reached a degree of barbarity more intense than in any other known system of slavery. The main features of the Putumayo system were strikingly akin to the Congo in its purpose—the production of rubber and its claim—that all the rubber of the forests was the property of alien speculators. Its methods, however, were slightly different. The Company made advances of European goods to the Indians, who then became debtors to the Company, who in turn appointed agents to force them to pay off the debts in rubber. The debts incurred were transferable and in the process of time became saleable assets. The sale of the debt assets in practice carried with it the bodies of the Indians. To apply this system a considerable force of soldiery was required to capture runaway debtors, and to compel the regular quotas of rubber. Indeed, it was found that the Company in London kept a record of armaments, which included in 1910 Winchester rifles alone to the value of £1,700. The evils of the system were accentuated, as in the Congo, by the payment of commissions to the heads of sections.

The Company's officers in Salisbury House issued a public statement that they declined to attach any credence to the allegations, and that they had the utmost confidence in Julio Cesar Arana. They refused on two occasions to see a deputation of British people who were concerned with the grave allegations made against this British registered Company. One of the chief officials, however, consented to see the representative of a newspaper, who put certain questions to him the replies to which he was told would be found in an envelope handed to him. The envelope handed to him contained a banknote! Thus did the Company, blind alike to their responsibilities and interests, endeavour to bluff public opinion.

But the publication of the Hardenburg papers and the ever-increasing pressure of public opinion at last compelled the Company to take official action, and two enquiries were set on foot: one by the British Government, and the other by the Company itself. The Government most concerned—that of Peru—remained singularly unmoved by the disclosures, and despite the treaty with Great Britain undertaking to prohibit all persons inhabiting its territory from taking any share in the slave trade, did nothing. The Peruvian Senate passed a resolution calling for an enquiry. The Government, to its lasting shame, ignored the demand.

The London Board of the Company still dallied with the situation, and only after a discussion lasting nine months did the directors decide to send out their own Commission of Enquiry. But even so it is doubtful whether this Commission would have arrived at the truth had it not been that Sir Edward Grey despatched the British Consul to watch the proceedings on behalf of British Barbadians employed by the Peruvian Amazon Company. It was thanks to this action and the presence of the British Consul that the whole story of this appalling crime was laid bare. Sir Edward Grey had faced for months the problem of intervention. It was one of extreme difficulty, for Great Britain had only limited treaty rights. Moreover, there were the susceptibilities of the United States to be considered. The British Government had reason for believing that the allegations were true, and that it could only be a matter of time before complete exposure was made. As many of the agents were British coloured subjects recruited in Barbados, there was ground at one time for believing that they would be made the scapegoats. It was in these circumstances that Sir Edward Grey was able to intervene and depute the nearest British Consul to report upon the work upon which these British subjects were engaged.

Just as in the case of the Congo, so in that of the Putumayo, the story of exploitation is written in letters of blood in the reports and documents of the perpetrators of the crime. When the appeal for winding up the Company was made in the Law Courts, Mr. Justice Swinfen Eady, while stating that the British Consul's report was no evidence, accepted the report of the Company's own officers, which, as he said, disclosed a disgraceful state of affairs.

> In practice, however, it produced abominable results from the commercial as well as from the humanitarian point of view. Misunderstanding and ill-feeling between the local managers and the Iquitos office appear to have been unceasing, and the managers both in Putumayo and Iquitos were at best criminally ignorant of the state of things obtaining in the huge territory that was subject to their administration.

Mr. Justice Swinfen Eady had no doubts as to the existence of slavery: 'Labour supervision as carried out by such men under the conditions above described and in the absence of any Governmental control rapidly became indistinguishable from slave-driving.'

He then described the absolute nature of the power wielded by the Peruvian Company:

> Absolute power was put into the hands of men who recognised no responsibility save that of extorting rubber for their own benefit. Forced labour of the worst sort, that imposed by fear by private individuals for their own benefit, was the basis. The Indians were considered as possessing none of the ordinary rights of humanity, women in particular would be assigned to employees on their arrival in a section.

Nothing could have been more clear and emphatic than the passages of the judgment dealing with the atrocities inflicted on the Indians:

> During the inspection worse crimes than those recorded were brought to light with the assistance of interpreters,

while no interpreters were needed to explain the marks visible on the backs of the men, women and children—marks it was hard to believe had not been impressed with a hot iron.

As the Editor of *Truth* said in one of his courageous exposures of the activities of the Company :

> They flog them (the Indians) inhumanly until their bones are laid bare ; they do not give them any medical treatment, but let them linger, eaten by maggots, till they die, to serve afterwards as food for the chiefs' dogs ; they mutilate them, cut off their ears, fingers, arms and legs ; they torture them by means of fire, of water, and by tying them up, crucified head down.

Those who wish to realise the intensity of the atrocities must read them in the evidence tendered by the Select Committee in the House of Commons. There are some things which cannot be published in a book of this nature. It was said of one of the supervisors of the Peruvian Amazon Company that

> He hunted, he kicked, and tortured to-day in order to terrify fresh victims for to-morrow . . . each crime led on to fresh crimes, and many of the worst men on the Putumayo fell to comparing their *battues* and boasting the number they had killed. Everyone of these criminals kept a large staff of unfortunate Indian women for immoral purposes. . . . The gratification of this appetite to excess went hand in hand with the murderous instinct which led these men to torture and kill the very parents and kinsmen of those they had cohabited with.

Another, Jermin Vasquez, boasted on his return from one district after he had carried out a series of beheadings that ' he had left the road pretty.'

> The lash spared none ; there was no pity for old men, women or children, all carry the ' mark of Arana,' and in more

than one case we hear of the whippers too tired to lift their arms again, passing on their whips to other men standing by impatiently waiting to continue the torture. All classes of the native population—young as well as old—women and children, youths and girls, casiques or capitanes, and their wives were marked, some lightly, others with broad and often terrible scars. . . .

The Editor of *Truth* summed up the kind of flogging which was inflicted upon the Indians who fell short in their rubber quotas. They were

frequently flogged to death; cases were reported to me where men and women had died actually under the lash. Salt and water would be sometimes applied to their wounds, but in many cases a fatal flogging was not even attended by this poor effort of healing, and the victim with maggots in the flesh was turned adrift to die in the forest, or was shot, and the corpse burned or buried.

The system as disclosed to the British public was one of robbery and outrage. Everything the Indian had possessed was taken from him—his gardens, his lands, his forest rights, his labour, and finally his own body; then in turn that of his wife and children. This wholesale robbery was imposed at the muzzle of the rifle and point of the bayonet. The miserable Indians were hunted into the forests; their dependents seized and outraged. Indeed, no deed was too bestial, no atrocity too revolting for the criminal agents of the Peruvian Amazon Company.

Arrayed against this system was the little band of those who had inherited the spirit of the Emancipators. They set out to smash up this nefarious undertaking, and rescue the Indians from their nightmare of suffering. They were confronted with scepticism, for their allegations against the Company seemed too ghastly to be true. They were ill-equipped with means, their efforts at securing evidence frustrated, but with undaunted spirit they accomplished their task.

The efforts made by Sir Edward Grey in association with the Government of the United States led firstly to the publication of a Grey Book which showed that for some years the Government of the U.S.A. had known in some detail of the horrors of the Putumayo; secondly, to a remonstrance by the United States Government to that of Peru. This Anglo-American action led to a semblance of activity, for more than 200 warrants for the arrest of the criminals were issued, but not a single person of any note was ever punished by the Peruvian Government.

The British House of Commons secured the appointment of a Select Committee under the chairmanship of Mr. Charles Roberts, which held 36 sittings in the House of Commons and received evidence from 27 witnesses, amongst whom were Julio Cesar Arana and Mr. Hardenburg. The Report of this Committee is a monument to the painstaking care with which every allegation was examined, and its conclusions are set forth in a series of paragraphs covering the principal features of the enquiry. Under the heading of Confirmation of Atrocities is the following pregnant paragraph:

> Your Committee did not consider that it fell within their province to investigate further into the truth of the atrocities stated to have been committed in the Putumayo. The details of these atrocities are set out in the Putumayo Bluebook. The accepted fact of the outrages was the starting point of their inquiry. Incidentally during the course of their

investigation the reality and the gravity of these atrocities have been admitted, established and confirmed.

There remained but one practical step—namely, that of securing the winding up of the Company. For this purpose a small group of shareholders placed in the hands of the Anti-Slavery Society the necessary powers, and on March 19, 1913, a petition for winding up the Company was presented to Mr. Justice Swinfen Eady and the petition succeeded. The concluding words of the judgment were as follows:

> I am quite satisfied upon the whole of the case, both with regard to the manner in which the operations of the Company were conducted in the Putumayo district and in Brazil, and with regard to the way in which the financial transactions in this country have been concerned, that it is a case in which there ought to be a Compulsory Order to be followed by the fullest investigation, and that Senor Arana is the last person to whom the conduct of that investigation ought to be allocated. Under these circumstances I make the Compulsory Order.

Thus was registered another triumph of justice and humanity over a great and terrible tragedy of slavery. For this triumph Mr. Charles Roberts was mainly responsible. He was not content to act as a figure-head Chairman of the Select Committee, but gave without stint his time and thought to the task of unravelling and exposing the truth, and searched through every document submitted to the Committee, visited Government departments and even the Company's offices in order to equip himself with every scrap of information which would assist the Select Committee in arriving at the truth, and in thereby liberating the Indians of South America from the really ghastly system of oppression under which they were suffering.

The work of Mr. Charles Roberts as Chairman of the Putumayo Select Committee formed one of the subjects of a book [1] published by *Truth* and written by the pen of a brilliant writer. Through the courtesy of the Editor I am allowed to publish certain extracts from his appreciation :

> Charles Roberts started life with almost everything against him—the son of a clergyman, a Balliol scholar, a tutor of Exeter College, and a violent teetotaller—it was much, very much for a rising politician to live down. . . . When this zealous young man was made chairman of the Putumayo Committee, old Parliamentary hands, as they say in Ireland, shook their heads. People of discretion pointed out that it would be just like Charles Roberts, in his impetuous way, to get at the truth which is not the function of the chairman. . . .
>
> Although it was quite irrelevant to the inquiry, he substituted a map of Peru for the usual whitewash. In his donnish way he began to pick up Spanish, which was also going far beyond the terms of reference. He allowed exhibits to be laid before the Committee which were distinctly rude, and for days at a time the room was as unpleasant a place of propaganda as the anti-vivisection shop in Piccadilly. Then there came that thrilling morning when he gorgonised Mr. Lowther, and, armed with a Speaker's warrant, charged down upon the Peruvian Amazon Company's offices, and, after collaring their books, returned triumphantly to Westminster with his taxicab groaning and howling under the weight of the booty. . . .
>
> In the meantime countless Indians on the Amazon and the Putumayo have reason to bless him in their prayers for as courageous an investigation of nameless horrors as stands to the credit of any Parliamentarian since the days of Shaftesbury and Plimsoll.

[1] 'Minor statesmen'—Viscount Peel, Lord Banbury, Lord Reading, Lord Milner, Lord Cecil, Josiah Wedgwood, Charles Roberts and others.

CHAPTER XII

The Servitude of Rubber and Cocoa—Portuguese Cocoa—Its Slavery and its Nemesis

St. Thomé Cocoa—The British Chocolate Firms—Sir Edward Grey's Action—Cadbury-Standard Case—Ross and Cramer.

When does Contract Labour become Slavery?—The answer is quite simple—when the person under Contract has been secured by force or fraud. For a hundred years natives of the African Continent have been shipped by the Portuguese from the mainland to their cocoa-producing islands of St. Thomé and Principe. The struggle for their freedom and for the reform of the labour systems in the territories of our 'Ancient Ally' has fallen mainly upon a handful of British subjects, with some help from a few Portuguese, Americans and Swiss. Those who have borne the main burden have been Joseph Burtt, William Cadbury, H. W. Nevinson, and to a lesser degree the author and his wife.

The centre of this tragedy, for it has been a human tragedy for a hundred years and now promises to move swiftly to an economic disaster, is the 'pearl of the Atlantic,' situated on the Equator and called St. Thomé, with its little sister island of Principe to the north.

St. Thomé owes its name to the fact that on St. Thomas' Day (December 21) of 1470, the island was discovered by a bold Portuguese navigator named Ioao de Santarem. The island is about 400 square miles in extent, approximately that of New York. It was 157 years after its discovery that the Portuguese commenced their modestly lucrative industry, the farming of sugar cane. In 1822, however, an enterprising planter with that love of nature which is one of the most attractive traits of the Portuguese introduced into Principe from Brazil an ornamental plant for his gardens. Twenty years later that ornamental plant, introduced by Jose Gomés, had spread itself over both islands and was beginning to pour forth an export of cocoa beans to Europe and America. Throughout the nineteenth century the plantations were extending everywhere until the islands were covered with cocoa trees. By 1910 the Portuguese planters were sending to Europe and America over 36,000 tons of cocoa annually.

But throughout that century the cocoa had been shipped from the islands to the accompaniment of the anguish of untold thousands of Africans, whilst the very highway from the coast to the heart of the African Continent was marked along its stretch of a thousand miles by the bleaching bones of countless slaves who had died on their way—'to hell,' as the natives called St. Thomé. How true it seemed to that little band of reformers that 'the mills of God grind slowly,' but at long last those mills are grinding 'exceeding small.' Nemesis has stricken the 'pearl of the Atlantic,' and the cocoa plants are being destroyed wholesale by a fatal disease.

In the early part of this century a gentleman called at Bournville to see Mr. Cadbury, and upon enquiry as to his business, disclosed that he had a cocoa plantation to sell in St. Thomé. It is understood that Messrs. Cadbury had no desire to buy a plantation, for they were content to purchase St. Thomé cocoa in the ordinary market, and that only because it was useful to mix with other qualities; however, they thought it well to read the documents left for their perusal, and one can imagine something of their astonishment to read the following item in the schedule of assets: '200 black labourers £3,550'! (That is, slightly less than £18 per head.)

Here was a disclosure indeed, here was evidence of the most damning kind that the current rumours of the prevalence of Portuguese slavery in West Africa had a substantial basis. The disclosure placed upon Cadbury Brothers a responsibility which they did not shirk, namely, to leave nothing undone to get at the whole truth, to find out beyond question the methods adopted to produce the cocoa of which they were using such large quantities in the Bournville factory.

On paper the Portuguese Contract Labour system left nothing to be desired; the form of labour was stated to be a voluntary contract under which the Serviçal was stated to be engaged for agricultural work. The natives of Africa, it was said, voluntarily agreed to go overseas to work in the islands for a period of three years, they joyously boarded the ships at the West African ports, and their three years on the islands were one blissful holiday, rewarded by short hours, good food and clothing, modern houses and substantial wages, then a return to their African homes with their accumulated earnings—on paper !

But on November 22, 1909, Sir Edward Grey invited the Portuguese Foreign Minister to come and see him, and told him what the British Foreign Office knew about the willingness or otherwise of the Africans going to the cocoa plantations. 'I explained to him,' says Sir Edward Grey, 'that the information I had received from private sources placed beyond doubt the fact that it had been the custom for natives to be captured in the interior by people who were really slave dealers.' Sir Edward Grey would not lightly charge the Portuguese Government with permitting slave-dealing, and in fact he is known to have possessed overwhelming evidence of these dreadful practices.

During the celebrated Cadbury *v.* Standard case in December, 1909, a good deal was made of the evidence upon what the Portuguese called 'recruiting,' but which the British Foreign Secretary called slave-dealing. Sir Edward Carson asked the Court whether Judge and Jury had ever heard in the world's history of worse conditions of slavery than in the Contract Labour system of Portuguese West Africa—'have you ever heard of conditions more revolting, more cruel, more tyrannous, and more horrible than what has been deposed to as regards the slavery in San Thomé ? Men recruited in Angola, women recruited in Angola, children recruited in Angola, torn away against their will from their homes in the interior, marched like droves of beasts through the Hungry Country, and when they are unable to walk along for a thousand miles to the Coast, shot down like useless dogs or useless animals, and others brought down to be labelled like cattle and brought over to San Thomé and Principe, never again to return to their homes.'

When Mr. Joseph Burtt, who had made a special study of the system on the spot, was being examined in court by Sir Edward Carson, he was asked:

> Then I may take it that your evidence here to the Jury is that you are satisfied that under the Serviçal system as it existed then, thousands of black men and women were against their will, and often under circumstances of great cruelty, taken away every year from their homes and transported across the sea to work on unhealthy islands from which they never returned?—Yes.

The Cadbury-Standard case produced overwhelming evidence that the 'Contract' systems in West Africa involved slave-trading, slave-raiding and slave-owning. The array of eminent Counsel was formidable and included Sir Rufus Isaacs (Lord Reading), Sir John Simon, and Sir Edward Carson (Lord Carson).

Thus some of the most brilliant legal minds in the kingdom were brought to bear upon conditions in Portuguese West Africa. It is, however, of first importance to realise that the actual existence of slave-owning and slave-trading was never once contested throughout the action. The issue before the Courts was the conduct of Messrs. Cadbury, but beyond question, if a clear case against slave-owning and slave-trading could have been established it would have been raised. It was never once raised, and moreover this body of eminent men were unanimous upon the point that the Portuguese Contract Labour was nothing but slavery, and Sir Edward Carson formally declared that this was common ground between Counsel:

My learned friend, Mr. Isaacs (Lord Reading) said in the course of his opening that the question of slavery in the Islands of San Thomé and Principe was not in issue in this action. Gentlemen, it is not an issue in one sense; it is not an issue in the sense that it is denied—it is admitted. . . .

The labourers had been secured by slave-raiding and slave-trading practices, and were held on the islands in bondage so rigid that 'none ever returned.' Lady Simon in her book 'Slavery' tells us that in the twenty years from 1888 to 1908 alone, over 67,000 natives were shipped to the Cocoa Islands and that: 'In spite of statements made by apologists—that at the termination of the Contract the labourers were repatriated—we know that practically none was ever allowed to return to the mainland from these Islands.'

Mr. William Cadbury, who made a personal enquiry into the subject, satisfied himself that during twenty years none of the contracted labourers had ever been allowed to go back to their homes by consulting the Curator at Novo Redondo in Angola, who 'informed us that on December 4th (1908) there returned to Novo Redondo from San Thomé on the s.s. *Malange* the first ten men ever repatriated.'

The Portuguese apologists insisted that the contracts were of limited duration. This contention was shattered by the British Consul, Mr. Drummond Hay, who visited the islands and then submitted a report to Sir Edward Grey in which he pointed out that he had examined at random a group of 'Contracts' numbering 163 (97 men and 66 women), that in only 28 cases was it possible to discover the years they had been kept on the islands, and that the average period the 28 had been in servitude upon the islands worked out at more than 31 years each.[1]

But the evidence given in the British Law Courts was only part of the volume of evidence which then and to this day unhappily still constitutes the indictment of the Portuguese labour system in West Africa. During the five years 1912 to 1917 the British Foreign Office issued a whole series of White Papers, the cumulative effect of which was overwhelming, and in addition to these Foreign Office papers there was a veritable cloud of witnesses. Lady Simon, commenting upon the recent report of two Americans, Messrs. Ross and Cramer, says: 'The allegations they make with regard to corruption or cruelty, or slavery under an alias, are but a repetition of accusations that have been made by a long line of reliable witnesses. Colonel Colin Harding found and disclosed a similar state of affairs in 1901 to 1902. In 1904–5 he was followed by a British journalist, Mr. H. W. Nevinson, who exposed the same evils of oppression and corruption in his book "A Modern Slavery." In 1908 to 1909 the Rev. Charles Swan told the same story in his book "The Slavery of To-day." Next, the veteran English missionary, Dan Crawford, who had lived in Angola since 1888, laid before the public his experiences in "Thinking Black." Then followed the enquiry instituted by the Cocoa Firms, Messrs. Cadbury, Fry, Rowntree and Stollwerck. Mr. Joseph Burtt, the Commissioner sent out by the firms, could only confirm with new details the old story. Then Mr. William Cadbury went out to West Africa and added his evidence in "Labour in Portuguese West Africa." These disclosures by administrators, jour-

[1] Cmd. 6322, p. 74.

nalists, missionaries, merchants and Consular Officers, have provided a mass of evidence, and the outstanding fact is that all the witnesses are in substantial agreement.'

The British public naturally feels a deep concern at the reports of slavery and analogous systems in Portuguese West Africa. This concern arises firstly because between our two countries there exist explicit treaty obligations for abolition; secondly, owing to the fact that our most ancient ally is joined to us by a peculiar relationship, which in turn obliges us to use the forces of Great Britain in defence of Portuguese territory. Upon this point the late Lord Cromer sounded a strong note of warning: 'There are some things that no British Government, however powerful otherwise, can undertake to perform. First and foremost amongst those things is the use of the war-like strength of the British Empire to maintain a slave state. In spite of the long-standing friendship between the two countries, in spite of historical associations which are endeared to all Englishmen, and in spite of the apparently unequivocal nature of Treaty engagements, it would, I feel assured, be quite impossible, should the African possessions of Portugal be seriously menaced, for British arms to be employed in order to retain them under the uncontrolled possession of Portugal so long as slavery is permitted.'

All the evidence from Portuguese West Africa points to a continuance of abuses, but for the time being shipments to the islands have practically ceased, for the 'Angel of Destruction' is sweeping through the islands, the plantations have been stricken with 'thrips,' a pest which is attacking the cocoa trees in both islands, and the former crop of 36,000 tons, worth £2,000,000, has dropped to the very low figure of about 9,000 tons of cocoa of doubtful value; the official bulletins make dismal reading, the Health Department records the prevalence of leprosy, elephantiasis, pneumonia and fever.

The mortality figures amongst the remaining labourers is no lower than it was eighteen years ago, but instead of labourers being imported from Africa, the Government is being compelled by the economic bankruptcy of the islands and the spread of disease to send thousands of the old Serviçal or slave population back to the African Continent.

The difficulties of the mainland are still to some extent linked with those of the Cocoa Islands. The most recent reports of any authority are those of Professor Ross and Dr. Cramer. These two American gentlemen were sent to Portuguese West Africa by a Committee which included such eminent men as George Foster Peabody, Raymond B. Fosdick, Joseph P. Chamberlain, James T. Shotwell and Hamilton Holt. The report of their investigations was issued in several countries, but there was really nothing new in what they said. There was the same story of corruption in the administration; the same allegations of theft from the wages of the contract labourers; there were also old and new forms of torture and oppression. One of the most striking features was the abundant evidence of corruption. As Professor Ross says, Colonial service in Portuguese colonies is less a career than a method of obtaining money. 'Why should they [the officials] look ahead and plan to promote the economic upbuilding of the country? They do not care for the country, they never expect to settle there. They care not even for the future of the Government which they represent. Their controlling thought is to make money before another is given their place. They realise it is theirs to "make hay while the sun shines."'[1]

The Portuguese made a feeble attempt to discredit the report of Messrs. Ross and Cramer. The usual line was taken of abusing the investigators, and again the usual Portuguese practice of issuing a whole series of pamphlets and legislation. It has frequently been said that it is quite impossible for any Portuguese judge to read, much less possess, a knowledge of the stream of legislation which has been issued from Lisbon during the last hundred years, but within recent times a Press Bureau has been created for the avowed purpose of trumpeting abroad any new legislation issued from Lisbon, one of the most amusing features of which is a laudatory preface which is now usually attached to any such legislation. One of the most recent issues contained as preamble the following:

> As a nation, Portugal wishes to call the attention of the world to the following statements regarding her national policy:
>
> (1) Portugal was the first nation to spread abroad in the world the high ideals which are the foundation of civilization.
>
> (2) Portugal has spent large sums of money in support of religious missions to raise the native races in accordance with the highest traditions of civilization.

It might have been added that some of the slaves, on being brought down to the coast, were baptised into the Christian faith!

[1] Para. 70, Ross' Report.

British criticism, which has now become international criticism, of Portuguese colonial methods, arises from no antipathy to the Portuguese as a nation—in point of fact the British critics have in their turn been criticised for their friendly attitude towards the Portuguese people. Certainly no one would rejoice more than the critics themselves if Portugal would cease to abuse her critics, stop the continuous issue of legislation which is seldom applied, and set about the task of real reforms in the administration itself. These friendly critics of Portugal undertook a special mission to Lisbon in November, 1910, in the hope of persuading the Government to bring about reforms which would be effectual in putting an end to abuses, but without avail.

Lady Simon in her book applies a twofold test to the Portuguese. It is known that the British Foreign Office made overtures to the Portuguese Government under which, if Portugal would reform her labour system, Great Britain on her part would do what she could in promoting a movement of free labour. It is also well known that the principal cocoa firms of Great Britain continue to refuse knowingly to purchase cocoa grown on Portuguese plantations. Lady Simon thus states these two challenging facts :

> The two striking facts which no consular despatch and no Portuguese excuse can get over are, first, that the reputable cocoa manufacturers of Great Britain have not withdrawn their boycott ; and, second, that the British Foreign Office, though prepared to recommend the withdrawal of the boycott by the cocoa firms, apparently has never yet been satisfied that the consular reports received from West Africa justify the British Government in carrying out its part of the 1913 bargain, under which our consular officials would feel free

to recommend labourers to enter into contracts for service with the Portuguese planters !

Until these two things happen, public opinion is surely justified in holding the view that Portuguese labour systems are barely, if at all, distinguishable from slavery.

CHAPTER XIII

Native Lands and British Policy

The Rival ' Heresies '—The Native Conception—Land Distribution—Lord Selborne's Dilemma—A Filibustering Agreement—The Struggle for Rhodesian Lands—The Judgment—South African Policy—The Kenya Expropriation—Kenya Distribution—Native Uneasiness—West African Policy.

The last fifty years have witnessed a relentless conflict between what have been called two land heresies. In British South and East African territories the white settler communities have denounced British West African land policy as a heresy, whilst in West Africa the policy adopted by the East and South of the Continent has been dubbed heretical with equal vigour. So far as a single sentence is capable of defining these opposing policies—whilst West African policy regards land as vested primarily in the ownership of the indigenous African, East and South Africa have asserted that priority in ownership should be vested in the immigrant races. The ethical forces associated with the names of Wilberforce and Buxton have never lost an opportunity for asserting that equity, common sense, economic and political stability are all inherent in the West African system, whereas the policy adopted in East and South Africa was bound to lead to most disastrous consequences.

To the African the supreme issue of life is his land; franchise, cattle, industry, labour and polygamy each involve their respective difficulties, but land overtops each and all of them. Take from the African his political or personal freedom, take his cattle, or even his wife and children, and he will tolerate the injustice, but touch his land and he will stake all in battle, no matter what the forces arrayed against him. Take the land, back the robbery with rifles, machine guns and 'heavies,' and the African will still face the 'bloody music' with primitive spear, bow and arrow. The terrible odds make the struggle hopeless, but as the African has said so many times in history, 'Take my land and you take my life'; therefore, he argues, as well lose life by bullet or cannon shell as by being robbed of land.

The European conception of the commercial ownership of land is totally alien to primitive native thought; a century ago almost any of the tribes in Africa would have looked upon the sale of tribal lands as an act of the most revolting kind. Land to the primitive African is one of the three component parts of his life. Sun, water, land, these represent to the native mind not three elements, but a single element, the supreme object of which is the provision of human sustenance. This machinery is so interdependent that the primitive African would be as horrified at the alienation and sale of land as at the sale of water or sun. It thus follows that the ownership of land is nowhere vested in the individual but in the whole race inhabiting a particular area, whilst every member of the tribe possesses as much right to the usage of adequate land as he does to the usage of an adequate share of the warmth of the sun or a draught of water from the local spring.

It might be assumed that such tribal ownership precludes immigrant settlers—it does nothing of the kind. It precludes monopoly, it shuts out self-interest it is true, but there are adequate means by which any man, no matter of what race, creed or colour, may obtain secure title to occupancy right of adequate land. The immigrant entering tribal areas would be confronted not with a question as to what land he requires and at what price, but with the initial question of whether or not he is a fit and proper person to become part of the tribal order. If it is decided that the immigrant is a suitable person to enter the community, the allotment of land follows as naturally as the gift of a wife, for the African believes it to be the first duty of man to multiply and replenish the earth.

The native systems and the principles of native land law are almost identical in the Central and Southern territories of the Continent, but in South Africa these have been subject to three centuries of dislocation under the pressure of the varying European systems of Dutch and British tenure, so that little remains but the hopeless confusion which to-day confronts the Union Government of South Africa.

Over the greater part of Africa this primitive conception has been shattered by the influx of the white races. Exploitation and the concessionaire have done their fell work of goading the native to rebellion and then confiscating his land rights. In some parts a hybrid system, partly European and partly African, has taken the place of the old one, but in a few areas efforts have been made by Great Britain to preserve all or nearly all of the best features of the original native land laws. In a very few territories primitive land laws still obtain untouched by inroads of European exploitation.

The following table demonstrates what is so often overlooked in connection with African problems, namely, the sparseness of the population:

(1)	Transkei (Cape Colony Native Reserve) ..	59	per	square	mile.
(2)	Nigeria	53	,,	,,	,,
(3)	Gold Coast (Colony) ..	50	,,	,,	,,
(4)	Basutoland	42·5		,,	,,
(5)	Uganda	33	,,	,,	,,
(6)	Nyasaland	31	,,	,,	,,
(7)	Tanganyika Territory..	11	,,	,,	,,
(8)	Kenya	11	,,	,,	,,
(9)	Northern Rhodesia ..	3	,,	,,	,,

The sparseness of African population is in striking contrast with the teeming millions of the East, for taking the nine great British areas in the above table, the density over the whole is only slightly in excess of 32 per square mile, compared with 226 per square mile in the British Provinces of India.

It must be remembered that African economic and social life depend largely upon ownership of cattle—cattle being used not only for sustenance but as a form of money, *e.g.* for obtaining wives. They require so much land that they may almost be said to eat up the ground; moreover, the African system of agriculture exhausts the soil very quickly, and for this reason more land is required per head in order to sustain existence than under the more intensive agricultural methods of

Europe and America. Sooner or later the question of improving the soil will have to be faced, and that boldly, by the responsible authorities.

To the everlasting honour of the Colonial Office every effort has been made to keep the ownership of land in West Africa in the hands of the tribes. It has not been easy to do so because again and again the worst sinners against the African race have been their own people; many a West Coast native has both unwittingly and wittingly betrayed his own people. But on the whole the British Colonial Office has been as successful in the West as it has been unsuccessful in South and East Africa and in certain areas in the South Seas.

Land belonging to native tribes has been systematically alienated by inveigling them into treaties and concessions, by inciting them to war, and by the application of administrative ordinances. The method of alienation by concession reached its most Gilbertian absurdity in Swaziland. When Lord Selborne[1] endeavoured to bring some order out of the chaos he discovered, in the first place, that every acre of land had been alienated to white men, and thus the native had nowhere to live. Next in confusion he found that concessions overlapped each other territorially; furthermore, that one white man had got the land, another had got the trees upon the land, while yet another had got everything under the land. In point of fact, these concessions went much further; to one white man certain taxes were conceded, to another telegraphs, to another road-making, and to yet another a trade monopoly. As Lord Selborne humorously remarked,

[1] Governor of Transvaal and High Commissioner for South Africa, 1905–1910.

'The number of concessions given were only limited by the available number of boxes of champagne!'

But the situation did not even end there, for one white man who arrived in Swaziland with the purpose of securing a concession, discovered this situation and obtained from the Swazis a concession which granted to him anything and everything that had not been granted to anybody else. But chaos did not end even there. Confusion was worse confounded owing to South African rivalries, through which both Great Britain and President Kruger for the Transvaal Government had agreed to recognise the validity of all these concessions!

The difficult task of unravelling the threads of this confusion was entrusted by the British Government to Mr. George Grey, brother of Viscount Grey, who it will be remembered met with so tragic a fate whilst hunting lions. The recommendations of Mr. George Grey were issued in 1906, and under these most of the Swaziland concessions were cancelled.

The greatest land case ever fought on behalf of natives by their friends in Great Britain was the Rhodesian Land Case of 1914–18. The stress of the Great War precluded the publicity which this historic struggle would have received. This case illustrated more clearly than perhaps any other the method of goading natives into war and then confiscating their land rights. The trivial incident of the alleged theft of a small piece of telegraph wire was the match that started the blaze of the Matabele War; the bait to the white settlers to go in and take the land is to be found in the secret agreement between Sir Starr Jameson and his troopers. Here it is:

(Copy certified.)

VICTORIA,
August 14, 1893.

Capt. Allan Wilson, Victoria.
SIR,

The following are the conditions of service for the members of the Victoria Force for Matabeleland.

1. That each Member shall have protection on all claims in Mashonaland until six months after the date of cessation of hostilities.

2. That each Member will be entitled to mark out a farm of three thousand morgen (6,000 acres) in any part of Matabeleland. No occupation is required, but a quitrent will be charged on each farm of ten shillings per annum.

3. That no marking out of farms and claims will be allowed or held valid until such time as the Administrator and the Commanders of the different columns consider the country sufficiently peaceful, and a week's clear notification will be given to that effect.

4. That Members be allowed four clear months wherein to mark out and register their farms, and that no such marking out or registration will be valid after that time with the exception of the rights belonging to Members of the Force killed, invalided, or dying on service.

5. The Government retain the right at any time to purchase farms from the Members at the rate of £3 (three pounds) per morgen and compensation for all improvements. This does not include the purchase of claims already pegged out on farms.

6. That any Member of the Victoria Force is entitled to 15 claims on reef and 5 alluvial claims. The Protections works to be: thirty feet shaft within six months, or sixty feet shaft within twelve months on reef claims. Alluvial claims are to be subject to existing laws in Mashonaland.

7. The 'loot' shall be divided one-half to the B.S.A. Company and the remainder to officers and men in equal shares.

8. Each man to be mounted and equipped, and rationed when practicable.

9. For the protection of Members of the Pioneer Force, no marking out of claims will be allowed on the part of fresh arrivals until four months have elapsed from the time specified in Clause 4.

10. From that date on which the Force crosses the Border, the rights of any Members of the Force dying, invalided or killed on service shall be protected and secured to his estate.

I have the honour to be, etc.

L. S. JAMESON,
for the B.S.A. Company.

Further Conditions.

11. That in the event of payable gold being discovered upon any farm, no mining or milling for a profit or flotation can take place until the farmers' rights are satisfied according to Clause 5, viz., of the rate of three pounds per morgen.

(Signed) L. S. JAMESON,
for the B.S.A. Company.

That document, assuredly unique and indeed disgraceful in British history, was secured in Rhodesia and brought back to this country by the author for the purposes of the case before the Privy Council.

In plain language, what did this document (the existence of which was long denied) involve?

It clearly provided for the invasion of Matabeleland. It offered the tempting bait of 6,000 acres of land to each invader, and it will be observed that under Clause 5 the bait was gilded with a pledge of £9,000 or £3 per morgen, which, with a promised 'equal share' of the loot (which could have hardly been worth less than £1,000), made a total potential gift of £10,000 to each of the 672 troopers taking part in the invasion. Or, otherwise stated, a total of £6,720,000. Indeed, if reference is made to the evidence of witnesses before Lord Cave's Commission in Rhodesia, this was stated to be the value attached by each invader to this agreement. It is no wonder that every effort was made both in South Africa and in London to keep secret the existence of this disgraceful document signed by Jameson on behalf of the British South Africa Company.

When the Attorney-General, Sir F. E. Smith, later Lord Birkenhead, opened the case for the British Crown before the Judicial Committee of the Privy Council he prefaced his speech by emphasising that the issues raised in this case were of the 'gravest conceivable importance' to the British Empire.

The Chartered Company, or, to give it its full title, the British South Africa Company, claimed that the entire lands of Southern Rhodesia not leased or sold to white men were the property of its shareholders. This claim meant that not a single native throughout the territory owned a foot of the land of his ancestors, and that by some means yet to be laid before the Judicial Committee of the Privy Council the 750,000 natives had forfeited all ownership rights to their lands. The British Crown and the white settlers were affected from the constitutional standpoint, whilst the native inhabitants of Rhodesia and other races within the British Commonwealth were vitally concerned in two other respects :

1. If the Chartered Company succeeded, the natives of Southern Rhodesia would be so completely divested of ownership that they could only remain in their country as mere occupants upon the lands of alien landlords.

2. The confirmation by the Judicial Committee of the Company's claim would thus involve the setting aside of that pillar of the British Constitution which

provides for the recognition of native customary law, particularly with reference to property rights.

This claim by the Chartered Company was of such an extraordinary nature that the Crown decided to oppose it. The white settlers of Rhodesia also entered a plea against a claim which threatened the future Government of Rhodesia, whilst it was arranged that Mr. Leslie Scott should appear and ask for permission to be heard on behalf of the natives. The preliminary hearing of the Reference took place on August 4, 1914, before the Lord Chancellor (Lord Haldane), Lord Dunedin, Lord Atkinson, Lord Moulton, Lord Sumner, and the Lord Chief Justice (Lord Reading).

The case for the natives rested upon the following main propositions :

1. The natives had never alienated their land rights.

(*a*) The only concessions given by Lobengula, the Matabele King, were restricted to minerals and waste lands.

(*b*) No concession could apply with equal force to both Mashonaland and Matabeleland, for these countries were inhabited by separate tribes and the Mashonas were 'friendly.'

2. The complete expropriation of the whole of the natives from their land rights would be an act without precedent in British colonial history.

3. The British Government has never by any formal act dispossessed the natives of their land rights.

(*a*) Rhodesia is not British territory [1] and the natives are not British subjects. The British Government is bound to the Matabele

[1] At that time.—J. H.

> and Mashona tribes by a treaty of Amity, and nothing in this treaty gives the Protecting Power the right to divest the *protected* natives of their land rights.

After a struggle lasting for four years, during which Mr. Carey Morgan, the solicitor for the natives, gave his time and his remarkable talents with prodigal liberality, the judgment was delivered on July 29, 1918, and it was of considerable length and not a little obscurity. From the native point of view the following words of Lord Sumner were a severe blow : 'Whoever now owns the unalienated lands, the natives do not.'

As 'unalienated' land meant all land not in the occupation of the white races it would be seen that the sentence quoted above, if it stood alone, stripped the inhabitants of the country—both Mashona and Matabele—of any rights whatsoever in their own country.

Of the three opponents of the Company, the Crown won most, in that legal title became vested in the British Crown as trustee for the inhabitants. The real position was best summed up in the following passage :

> Their Lordships think it sufficient to say that, except in so far, if at all, as the rights of the Crown are subject to those of the Natives and the Company, nothing has been shown to have happened or to have been done, that would prevent the Crown, if and when the Company's tenure of the administration of Southern Rhodesia determines, from disposing of the lands then remaining unalienated by any lawful means and in favour of any persons or purposes, as it may duly be advised. . . .

The natives came an easy second to the Crown.

The white settlers received but scant attention in the judgment. In the first place the natives gained the enormous advantage of finding that the lands they occupied were no longer under the control of the Chartered Company's shareholders but under the direct control of the Crown, for as will be observed from the above passage, Crown rights were subject to indigenous requirements.

There was also the further advantage to the natives that Crown ownership removed from them the perpetual menace of a commercial temptation to cut down their reserves. Prior to the judgment, the Company's claim to the commercial ownership of the reserves meant that it was always in the interest of the Company to make out a case for cutting off the best portions of the reserves, and the natives were thus constantly exposed to the threat of eviction; indeed, whilst the case was proceeding, it had been decided to evict the natives from 6,000,000 acres of reserves and place them elsewhere on 5,000,000 acres.

The Company came off worst, for it completely lost its case. Some of the passages in the judgment might well be handed down to history as a warning to concessionaire companies of the danger of over-reaching themselves. Dealing with the claim advanced by the Company in connection with the Lippert Concession, upon which the Company's case rested, Lord Sumner said that the Company contended that:

> He (Lobengula) granted to him (Lippert) all the right of dealing with land of which he had any knowledge, and his ignorance of the nature of an estate in fee ought not to derogate from the amplitude of a grant, which was as wide as he knew how to make it. He reserved at any rate nothing

but money considerations for himself, and when the Lippert and the Rudd concessions fell into the same hands, the King had, in substance, sold his country out and out to the Company. Their Lordships cannot accept this argument. As well might it be said that a savage who sold ten bullocks, being the highest number up to which he knew how to count, had thereby sold his whole herd, numbering, in fact, many hundreds.

Lord Sumner, in a passage which it would be hard to beat, showed the *reductio ad absurdum* of the Company's claim :

It would follow from the Company's claims that Herr Lippert was, or could become at pleasure, owner of the entire kingdom—for nothing is reserved in favour of the inhabitants —from the kraals of the King's wives to his father's grave or the scene of assembly of his indunas and his pitso. Thenceforward the entire tribe were sojourners on sufferance where they had ranged in arms, dependent on the good nature of this stranger from Johannesburg even for gardens, in which to grow their mealies, and pastures, on which to graze their cattle. The Lippert concession may have some value as helping to explain how and why the Crown came to confer the administration of Southern Rhodesia upon the Company, but *as a title deed to the unalienated lands it is valueless.*

That sentence put an end to the claims of the British South Africa Company.

The native areas in Southern Rhodesia were made into reserves and then formally vested in the High Commissioner in South Africa for the use and benefit of natives only. But the High Commissioner is debarred from alienating any of this land except for certain limited purposes, and then only in exchange for other land. The 'limited purposes' are mineral development, railways, and other public works and sites for townships required for the working of 'important minerals.' The lands of Southern Rhodesia held to-day in round figures are as follows:

The total area is 96,000,000 acres. The 1,000,000 natives hold as definitely reserved areas nearly 22,000,000 acres. The 50,000 European settlers hold about 33,000,000 with a right to take up altogether 48,000,000 acres. The remainder is held by the Crown for future allotment.

The decision of the Judicial Committee of the Privy Council was followed, as we have seen, by the adoption of a policy of racial separation of land occupation (not ownership), and this brought the native land policy of Southern Rhodesia into harmony with that of South Africa which had been inaugurated by General Botha in 1913. The land policy of South Africa was based upon the recommendations of Sir Godfrey Lagden's Commission, which sat from the years 1903 to 1905. General Botha, then both Prime Minister and Minister for Native Affairs, decided in 1913 to divide up the 300,000,000 acres of land in South Africa between white, coloured and native races, and he took as the guiding lines of his policy the four main land recommendations of the Lagden Commission:

(1) That in the interest of both Europeans and natives, purchase of land by natives should be limited to certain areas to be defined by legislative enactment.

(2) That whatever principles govern the question of purchase of land by natives should apply equally to the leasing of land by natives.

(3) That unrestrained squatting of natives on private farms, whether as tenants or otherwise, is an

evil, and that the principles of the Cape Act of 1899 should be adopted for dealing with it.

(4) That purchase of land which may lead to tribal or communal or collective possession of land by natives, as opposed to individual ownership, should not be permitted.

Under the Botha Scheme the following was the proposed distribution of land in acres:

		Present.		Future.	
	Population.	*Total Occupancy.*	*Per Native Capita.*	*Scheduled Areas.*	*Per Native Capita.*
(*a*) Cape Colony	1,900,000	13,000,000	7	16,200,000	8½
(*b*) Transvaal	1,200,000	2,400,000	2	13,500,000	11¼
(*c*) Natal	1,000,000	6,100,000	6	10,200,000	10
(*d*) Orange Free State	350,000	163,000	$\frac{4}{9}$	489,000	1½

The Botha Scheme was admittedly provisional, but the haste with which it was driven through Parliament and the premature eviction of natives from land then occupied by them led to a storm of protest.

The alarm and the unnecessary trek of the native squatters led to the infliction of much hardship and suffering. The missionaries, although divided upon the wisdom of the measure according to their individual comprehension of its provisions, but justly indignant at the sufferings caused by the premature application of the policy, did their best to dissipate prevailing ignorance and to mitigate the hardships by direct personal and collective appeals to the Government at home, knowing, however, that little could be done because the Imperial Government had promptly accorded its sanction to the principle of the 1913 legislation.

Although the natives were profoundly disturbed and were indeed showing signs of unrest, they did not oppose the bedrock principle of the legislation, for in their official communication to the South African Government the President of the South African Native Congress said, in an appeal for postponement of the measure and for further safeguards for native rights :

'We make no protest against the principle of separation so far as it can be fairly and practically carried out.'

General Botha endeavoured to assuage indignation in South Africa by giving frequent assurances both to the natives and to white public opinion, and formally declared :

(1) That legislation would be introduced for *gradual* expropriation of land held by any white man or native.

(2) Legislation would provide secure title both for collective and individual ownership.

(3) The Native Councils would be created for dealing with purely native affairs.

The land policy of General Botha has been described as the policy of the White and Black Checker Board, under which the whole of South Africa was to be divided up into black and white squares. If white people were found in the ' black squares ' they were to be moved as in a game of draughts to the ' white squares,' and natives in the ' white squares ' into the black areas. Its stages were first the Lagden Commission of 1903–5, then the Botha Legislation of 1913, and thirdly, the appointment of Sir William Beaumont's Commission. To this Commission was allotted the task of recommending steps to give practical effect to the legislation. The Commission sat for two years. When its report was published some months later, it recommended that the land to be placed ultimately in ' black squares ' should be increased by nearly 20 million acres of land, and the final result in practice will be that the South African ' black squares ' will be 40 million acres for nearly 5 million natives and the ' white squares ' will represent 260 million acres for about 1 million whites. A distribution so grotesquely inequitable that it must continue to be a source of justifiable unrest throughout the Union of South Africa.

Kenya to most colonial minds is a challenging issue in Empire policy. The political demands of the Kenya settlers are as simple as they are bold—namely, that whatever changes are made in the Constitution of East Africa the 3,000 permanent British settlers must at all times and in all ways possess a clear and dominant majority in the Legislature over all other British subjects, who number to-day at least 2,500,000.

The land policy of the Kenya settlers is equally simple and was boldly set forth by their spokesman, Lord Delamere :

' If the policy was to be continued that every native

was to be a landholder of a sufficient area on which to establish himself, then the question of obtaining a satisfactory labour supply would never be settled.'

To the natives of Kenya the question of land dominates all other issues. There seems to be no doubt that whatever native rights existed have been expropriated. Mr. Ormsby-Gore has affirmed this quite categorically in the Report of his Commission:[1]

'The legal position appears to be that no individual native and no native tribe as a whole has any right to land in the Colony which can be recognised by the Courts.'

This complete expropriation of native rights is not based upon conquest, finds no excuse in 'native rebellion,' for none has taken place, and is not the legitimate fruit of purchase or even compensation.

It was probably due to the stress of the Great War that this expropriation was carried through without any public notice of such a far-reaching measure. In the year 1915 a Crown Lands Ordinance was issued with the approval of the Colonial Office, the effect of which was set forth in the judgment in the Kikuyu Land Case before the High Court in 1921:

> In my view [said the presiding Judge], the effect of the Crown Lands Ordinance, 1915, and the Kenya (Annexation) Order in Council, 1920, by which no native rights were reserved, and the Kenya Colony Order in Council, 1921, as I have already stated, is clearly, *inter alia*, to vest land reserved for the use of the native tribe in the Crown. If that be so, then all native rights in such reserved land, whatever they were under the Gethaka system, disappeared, and the natives in occupation of such Crown land became tenants at will of the Crown of the land actually occupied.

[1] Cmd. 2387, 1925.

The Ormsby-Gore Commission of 1924 was followed by another under Sir Edward Hilton Young, and this Commission was in turn followed by the visit and report of Sir Samuel Wilson. The work of these Commissions was examined and consolidated in 1930–31 by the Joint Select Committee of both Houses of Parliament upon closer union in East Africa. This Committee sitting in the House of Lords was composed of ten Members of the House of Lords and an equal number of Members of the House of Commons. The Committee included the late Lord Stanley of Alderley as its first Chairman, Lord Passfield, Lord Cranworth, Lord Lugard, Mr. L. S. Amery, Mr. Charles Buxton, Sir Robert Hamilton, Lord Stanley and Mr. Ormsby-Gore. There was thus no lack either of talent, experience or authority.

What was the land position of Kenya when the Joint Select Committee was appointed? The best available material is supplied by Mr. Ormsby-Gore in his Report. It is important to bear in mind that the land policy adopted in Kenya must be to a considerable extent the key to any East African Land Settlement. The distribution is as follows:

(*a*) Native Reserves in Colony	..	46,837 sq. miles
(*b*) Forest Reserves in Colony	..	2,980 ,, ,,
(*c*) Land surveyed into farms	..	11,859 ,, ,,
(*d*) Area of Protectorate ..	..	2,200 ,, ,,
(*e*) Coast Province Extra Protectorate		13,980 ,, ,,
(*f*) Jubaland	..	36,740 ,, ,,
(*g*) Northern Frontier Province	..	92,180 ,, ,,
(*h*) Turkana	..	7,920 ,, ,,
(*i*) Remaining area	..	30,364 ,, ,,
Total	..	245,060 ,, ,,

The white population is to-day about 12,000, of whom less than 3,000 are settlers. The Indian population numbers about 25,000, of whom most are colonists. The natives are about 2,500,000.

It will be seen from the foregoing table that whilst the natives outnumber the immigrant white and coloured races by more than 2,400,000, there is reserved for them only 47,000 square miles out of a total of 245,000 square miles.

Under the land expropriation by the Ordinance of 1915, and the consequent removals, the natives of Kenya Colony had become increasingly nervous even as to their occupancy rights in the reserves, for as Mr. Ormsby-Gore said :

> There is probably no subject which agitates the native mind to-day more continuously than the question of their rights in land, both collectively as tribes and individually as owners or occupiers. In this disquiet they are actively supported in their claims by the missionary bodies of all denominations. Uncertainty in regard to future land policy is certainly the principal cause of disquiet among the natives, more particularly of Kenya and Nyasaland.

It was emphasised by successive Commissions, and realised by the general public not only in England but in Kenya, that this situation could not be prolonged without real danger in East Africa, and it was decided in 1930 to vest the native areas in a formal Trust. These lands were so vested that they were declared to be *for the use and benefit of the native tribes for ever.'*[1] The natives could not lease any of the land, but the Governor might do so under certain very rigid conditions, but even then only after submitting the proposal

[1] Italics mine.—J. H.

to the Native Councils. Then followed the usual clause with regard to the minerals previously declared to be the property of the Kenya Government—namely, that if the Government should so lease any reserve land it could only be done on condition that an equivalent area were added to the native reserve area. There was also to be compensation for disturbance.

But the Joint Select Committee of 1930–31 was obviously uneasy, for in their recommendations upon the land question they urged upon the Colonial Secretary that :

> In view of the nervousness among the native population as regards the land question, a full and authoritative enquiry should be undertaken immediately into the needs of the Native population, present and prospective, with respect to land within or without the reserves, held either on tribal or on individual tenure. Pending the conclusion of this enquiry, no further alienation of Crown land to non-natives should take place except in exceptional cases with the sanction of the Secretary of State.

Alas, how soon were their obvious misgivings to be justified, for within three years legislation was introduced into and passed by the Legislative Council of Kenya Colony for the variation of the Trust in order to permit of the winning of gold in the native reserve areas, and that without the promised reference to the Native Councils.

With such a land record in Kenya Colony it can be no matter for surprise that the Joint Select Committee found strong aversion in neighbouring territories not only by the natives, but by white people, to any proposal to unite in ' closer union ' Uganda, Tanganyika or Nyasaland with Kenya, for as they said in the Report :

Both European settlers and Chambers of Commerce have expressed themselves as adverse to the making of any constitutional changes at the present moment of economic difficulty. The European witnesses from Uganda, both official and unofficial, consider that any union with Kenya would be most unpopular, and the native evidence was very hostile to it.

It is to be hoped that the Kenya settlers will learn from colonial history that again and again it has been demonstrated that the march alike of freedom and of justice cannot be arrested.

If West African land policy be heresy, it has priceless advantages without which East Africa can never be peaceful or prosperous—two of which are contentment among the native population, and co-operative effort in political and industrial progress between white and coloured people. What is that West African 'heresy'? The West African 'heresy,' as it is often called by East African settlers, is set forth with authority and in all its fullness by Lord Lugard in his masterly work, 'The Dual Mandate.' The guiding principles of the policy begin with the conception that 'the land belongs to the people' of the Colony and that the duty of the chiefs is to act as trustees. It then becomes the function of the Administration to see to it that this trust is carried out honestly. In the early chapters of this book emphasis has been placed upon what were at the time regarded as the 'visionary' principles of Buxton and his colleagues. In point of fact those 'visionary' principles were so instinctively sound that fifty years later the fundamental theories of Fowell Buxton were being put into practice by Sir John Rodger, Sir Hugh Clifford and Lord Lugard.

These principles reposed upon a right conception of relationship between white and coloured people—namely, that the African was at his best as a producer and a merchant, and not as a servile labourer. To give a definite illustration. The West African 'heresy' has covered the Gold Coast Colony and a large part of Nigeria with native cocoa plantations capable of supplying the whole world with cocoa at a price which gives these colonies a prosperity without parallel in colonial history. The East African 'heresy' forbids to the native the right to grow coffee on any land occupied by himself and his family! Lord Lugard first gives a picture of the native mind with which every student of Africa, and indeed, of most other primitive regions, will be familiar:

'To the native mind, uninfluenced by foreign ideas, land is an unsaleable thing. "We have power to dispose of the land; we cannot sell the land; no chief can sell the land," said a Lagos chief in evidence before the Supreme Court.'[1]

The West African policy next accepts the doctrine of Trusteeship, under which the Governor becomes the trustee and must only allow land transactions to take place within the limits of native law and custom, as Lord Lugard says:

When a European Power succeeds to the domination hitherto wielded by a native conquering race, the control of the land, in so far as it was exercised by the latter, passes, if publicly claimed, to the new suzerain, and should be exercised in accordance with native law and custom. If the dominion was not vested in a conquering race, the controlling Power

[1] Cd. 5103, p. 32.

should interfere still less with customary law. Private and communal rights must be respected.

But the function of government does not stop with this guardianship of native land rights; the West African policy has always meant in practice 'the encouragement of small holdings, and their preservation against absorption in large estates, or alienation for debt; the utilisation of the land to the best advantage by permanent improvements; and the curtailing of shifting cultivation.'

The Administration of course possesses the right to take charge of *bona fide* vacant lands, and lands not in beneficial occupation, but as Lord Lugard says, this should only be done in the capacity of trustee and the proceeds from any development of waste land must be devoted to the public services.

It may be objected that such a land system debars the stranger from overseas from placing his energies and capital at the disposal of the Colony. It does nothing of the kind. The first principle of native ownership precludes the sale of the freehold, and quite properly so, because it is fundamental to native law and custom that the ownership shall not be alienated. Lord Lugard places the strangers seeking native land into a threefold category:

(*a*) those who intend to identify themselves with the tribe, and by inter-marriage become merged into it in the second generation (these require no special protection);

(*b*) those who settle on the land, but remain aliens to the tribe, and

(*c*) land speculators, who are generally absentee landlords, and may perhaps have acquired title to land from a chief who had no right under native law to grant it, but did not understand the effect of the deed—probably drawn by a native lawyer—conferring individual ownership.

Native law and custom which is embedded in British West African legislation provides for class (*a*) and class (*b*), but every effort has been made to exclude from the West African Colonies those who come under class (*c*). The Colony of Kenya has reversed the order—pride of place has been given to class (*c*), namely, the land speculator, whilst little encouragement has been given to classes (*a*) and (*b*), who are primarily concerned with linking themselves in friendly and loyal co-operation with progressive natives and tribes.

If British East African land policy is theoretically sound, it cannot be denied that it is a pretty bankrupt one in practice.

If British West African land policy is a 'heresy,' then it is a sound economic heresy for all concerned in its usage.

CHAPTER XIV

National to International Effort

First Anti-Slavery Treaties—The Asiento—Payments to Portugal and Spain—Castlereagh and Wellington—The Berlin Conference—The Brussels Conference—The Versailles Conference—The League of Nations—Britain and Piracy—Adoption of British Proposals—International Responsibility—The International Machine—Public Opinion.

The recent decision of the League of Nations to adopt the British proposals for committing the task of the Abolition of Slavery and the Emancipation of the Slaves to an International Expert Commission under the Council of the League of Nations was a signal triumph for the British Foreign Office. For nearly three hundred years successive British Governments have devoted an appreciable portion of their time and energy to the conclusion of treaties intended to suppress slavery in one or other of its many forms.

One hundred and fifty years before the British Abolition of the Slave Trade in 1807, the British Foreign Office was beginning the work of international abolition. From 1662 onward, treaties were being signed with this end in view. The first of these treaties was of restricted compass and designed only to protect British subjects :

That if any ship of Algier, Tunis, or Sally, or any other, do bring any ships, men, or goods, belonging to any of the subjects of His Majesty the King of Great Britain, &c., into Tripoli, or any of the ports thereto belonging, the Governors there shall not permit them to be sold within the said territories; and for the time to come, that no subjects of His said Majesty be bought or sold, or made slave of, in Tripoli or its territories.

Five years later a further treaty was made which provided asylum for escaping Christian slaves and absolved their protectors from any claim for compensation. The infamous Asiento agreement in the reign of Queen Anne was a retrograde step, but before the eighteenth century was over Wilberforce, Wesley, Clarkson and Sharp were stirring the national conscience, and throughout the nineteenth century the growth of public opinion against slavery in Great Britain generated intense activity on the part of the British Foreign Office. During the hundred years following the British decision to abolish the slave trade, successive British Governments concluded nearly 600 treaties and international instruments designed either to check or abolish the slave trade. (Eighty of these treaties were between Great Britain and Portugal.)

The crusading zeal of Great Britain succeeded by these treaties in making the slave trade internationally illegal over a large area of the world—on paper at least. But it is a surprising fact that during the period following the Napoleonic Wars no single statesman on the international stage appears to have grasped the fundamental fact that slave-*trading*, though illegal, could not be suppressed unless and until slave-*owning* was also abolished.

For the Abolition of Slavery in French possessions

in 1848 a good deal of credit must be given to the pressure which successive British Governments, urged on by the Anti-Slavery movement in this country, brought to bear upon French Governments, and more particularly to the valuable influence of the French Anti-Slavery Society upon Continental public opinion.

It is interesting to note that in 1841 Chili, and in 1848 Brazil, decreed slave-trading to be piracy. Though the execution of the decrees was lamentably defective, the attempt made by those Governments was at least better than the obstructive attitude maintained by the Governments of France, Italy, Spain and Portugal to this day against labelling slave-trading as piracy. Our own country has pressed steadily from 1815 to the present day for an international declaration of slave-trading as piracy, together with mutual right of search in the case of suspected slave ships, and on both points we have met with much opposition. France conceded the mutual right of search in 1833, but her action was greatly weakened by the stipulations which accompanied it.

Great Britain had uphill work in her efforts to induce Spain and Portugal to suppress the Slave Trade. The attitude of these countries was described by the Anti-Slavery Society in 1837 as 'the insulting indifference which the Governments of Spain and Portugal have shown in regard to the performance of their engagements.'

Portugal accepted from the British Government a gift of £300,000, and the cancellation of a loan of £600,000, and undertook in return to adopt certain measures towards the abolition of the Slave Trade. In return for the 1817 Treaty the British Treasury paid the Spanish Government £400,000 as compensation for the capture of certain slave ships. The payment of these large sums to Spain and Portugal is the more striking when it is remembered that at this period British coffers had seldom been more empty. But, to quote the Anti-Slavery Society once more, both these countries, 'having taken our money, turned a deaf ear to every remonstrance we have made.'

Lord Palmerston made characteristically vigorous protests. He declared that our ally had conformed to 'not one single restriction' imposed by her treaties, that she was still kidnapping and shipping negroes, and that she had no longer (Brazil being now an independent State) the excuse of any national or colonial interest. In his vivid language: 'The ships of Portugal now prowl about the ocean, pandering to the crimes of other nations, and when her own ships are not sufficiently numerous for the purpose, her flag is lent as a shield to protect the misdeeds of foreign pirates.' As this exceedingly outspoken remonstrance had no effect, Lord Palmerston took the internationally amazing but effective step of carrying through Parliament a Bill providing for the seizure by British ships of Portuguese vessels and other vessels not 'justly entitled to claim the protection of any State' if found equipped for the Slave Trade.

Lord Palmerston would have fluttered the dovecotes of Geneva to-day! But there are times when the Abolitionists of the present day would give a good deal to have amongst them the spirit of 'Pam,' in action as direct as in language outspoken.

The first stage in collective international effort was the Conference at Vienna in 1814, from which, as

Professor Coupland has pointed out, William Wilberforce hoped to obtain a 'Charter of Abolition' signed by all the European States.

The principal opponent of international action throughout history has been Portugal, whose opposition was as unbending in the years 1926 to 1931 at Geneva as it had been in 1815 at Vienna.

Lord Castlereagh had on his side at Vienna the vague but genuine idealism of the Czar Alexander, and he had also, thanks to Wellington's earlier efforts in Paris, the support of Talleyrand, but it is to be feared that most of the Powers regarded Abolition of Slavery as a strange British obsession, rather than a subject about which practical statesmen could be expected to concern themselves seriously. Castlereagh, however, though formerly an opponent of Abolition, fought tenaciously and well, and although the Spanish Government joined the Portuguese in their obstruction he was able to secure the signatures of the Eight Powers to an international instrument which provided for the universal abolition of the Slave Trade as quickly and effectually as possible. Even if to some foreign Governments this instrument represented little more than a pious wish, it was a step forward.

The ostensible ground of Portuguese objection to the reciprocal right of search of vessels has always been that it would be such an infringement of sovereign rights that incidents causing unpleasant friction between friendly Powers would be of frequent occurrence. Caustic critics sometimes suggest that the 'incidents' would indeed be 'unpleasant' to certain Portuguese subjects! Thus, when the Verona Conference met in 1823 the Duke of Wellington was again unsuccessful, for although France and Russia were ready for definite action, the opposition was too strong for the Iron Duke.

Slave-owning America would not hear of the right of search, and slave ships found shelter under the Stars and Stripes until the year 1862, and then at last began that British-American co-operation from which has accrued such substantial results. The Anglo-American Treaty conceded a mutual, if limited, right of search to British and American vessels, and the creation of Mixed Courts on both the African and American Coasts.

In 1841 an Anti-Slave-Trade Treaty was concluded between Great Britain, Austria, Prussia and Russia.[1] Article 1 engaged the high contracting parties 'to prohibit all trade in slaves under their respective flags; or by means of capital belonging to their respective subjects, and to declare such traffic piracy.' Unfortunately the treaty provided that the mutual right of search should not be exercised within the Mediterranean Sea. There were diplomatic reasons for excluding the Mediterranean, but it was well known that these waters were regularly used for the transit of domestic slaves and negroes on their way to the slave markets of Turkey.

So far as words were concerned, nothing could have been more satisfactory than the promises made by the Ottoman Porte to Lord Strafford de Redcliffe in 1857, promises which proved to be nothing more than 'words, idle words.'

Beaconsfield and Salisbury refused to bring the

[1] France signed the Treaty, but in the following year she refused to ratify it, objecting to the provision for the right of search.

question of slavery in Turkey before the Berlin Congress of 1878, and bolstered up ' the sick man of Europe ' without taking the opportunity to urge him, in return for the support of the Powers, to suppress slavery. It is true that an unsatisfactory convention for putting down slave-trading was concluded between Great Britain and Turkey in 1880, but the leaders of the Anti-Slavery movement were bitterly disappointed that the opportunity offered at Berlin was not taken.

The Conference at Berlin in 1885 was the next important stage in collective international action and secured seventeen signatures, but it was limited in its geographical operation to the conventional area of the Congo. This included the basin of the Congo and defined areas watered by the Loge, Zambesi, Ogowe, the Nile and the Niger, and Lake Tanganyika. Freedom of trade, protection of native rights and interests, the suppression of the Slave Trade and the encouragement of missionary enterprise all became an international concern.

The Brussels Act of 1890, like the Berlin Act, incorporated measures designed to protect the aboriginal populations of Africa, and it was the misfortune and not the fault of the signatories that one of the results of the two Conferences was the creation of the Congo Free State. The States attending the Conference numbered seventeen, and included not only the plenipotentiaries of the United States of America but also those of Turkey, Zanzibar and Persia. The Brussels Act provided for cruiser control of certain waters and the opening up of main roads to permit of the rapid movement of flying columns. Missionaries were to be protected and private organisations invited to co-operate in the repression of the Slave Trade. The arms traffic was prohibited, but whilst this made some difficulties for the Arab slave raiders, it led to the disarmament of the Congo natives, which in turn, alas, facilitated their enslavement. The Act also provided for the detention of suspected vessels and the conditions under which ships' officers could be brought to trial. It was under this Act that for the first time international offices for the collection of information were created. These were established at Zanzibar and Brussels.

The Brussels Conference was largely due to the persevering efforts of the British and Foreign Anti-Slavery Society, and partly the result of a motion proposed in the House of Commons in March, 1889, by Mr. Sydney Buxton, M.P. (now Earl Buxton) and seconded by Sir John Kennaway. The speakers hoped for the following results from the Conference: that the status of slavery should be no longer recognised by international law; that slave-trading should be declared equivalent to piracy; that all nations should allow the mutual right of search of suspected ships; and that the import of arms into Central Africa should be restricted. The proposal for mutual right of search provoked the usual violent opposition from France.

The year 1919 witnessed the opening of a new chapter, one destined to lead to a far-reaching movement. In this year the Powers than assembled for the Versailles Conference were led to consider the whole question of native races, and the British Government invited Sir Thomas Fowell Victor Buxton and the author to go to Paris—just a hundred years after the first Thomas Fowell Buxton went to Westminster as the Member of Parliament for Weymouth!

But 'Sir Victor'—as he was affectionately known—like his great-grandfather, passed away prematurely, being only fifty-four years of age. A motor accident which at first involved only temporary incapacity proved rapidly fatal, and his place in Paris was taken by Lord Henry Cavendish Bentinck.

The Convention of St. Germain was framed for signature by the Governments of the U.S.A., British Empire, Belgium, France, Italy, Japan and Portugal. It is interesting to note that the British Dominions and India signed it as separate States. The object of the Convention was that of revising the Berlin and Brussels Acts—the revision in fact opened the way to a wider field of service for native races. The obligations of the Berlin Act to bring about the 'suppression of slavery and especially the slave trade' became in the Convention of St. Germain 'the complete suppression of slavery in all its forms and of the slave trade by land and sea.'

The Convention, having extended its ethical objective far beyond the bounds of all previous treaties, proceeded to invite all State Members of the League of Nations to adhere to each beneficent obligation, and finally the Convention was linked with the League Covenant. Three years later began what may be best described as the Parliamentary work at Geneva. Foremost in this new endeavour were Sir Arthur Steel-Maitland, Lord Cecil and Dr. Nansen. Lord Lugard and Dr. Gohr of Belgium commenced what proved to be many years' work on League Commissions. Upon the late Mr. Harold Grimshaw devolved the heavy task, nobly discharged, of preparing the 'documentation' on behalf of the Secretariat of the League of Nations and the International Labour Offices.

It was in 1922 that Sir Arthur Steel-Maitland, then the representative of the Government of New Zealand, raised the whole question of slavery in the Assembly of the League of Nations. It was not an easy task, for he met with a good deal of opposition, but with the assistance of the members of the British Empire Delegation, and of Dr. Nansen, he carried the proposal that the League should commence the work of the suppression of slavery in all its forms. In due course the League Council appointed a temporary Slavery Commission, and instructed it to gather together for the information of the League all available material upon slavery questions. This Commission, of which Dr. Gohr was Chairman and Lord Lugard the British representative, issued its Report in 1925, and in the Assembly of the League that year the British Government presented for consideration the draft of a new Convention. This Convention had been prepared by the British Foreign Office in conjunction with other departments, and the Delegation under the leadership of Sir Austen Chamberlain formally presented it for acceptance by State Members of the League. The Convention ultimately adopted and still further enlarged the circumference of the work. It first recited the objects of the Convention of St. Germain and the General Act of Berlin and the General Act of Brussels, namely, 'the securing of the complete suppression of slavery in all its forms and of the slave trade by land and sea'; the Convention also undertook the prevention of forced labour from developing into conditions analogous to slavery.

The Convention contains twelve articles under which Slavery and the Slave Trade are both defined. Article 5, which deals with certain forms of forced labour, is new in international treaties and places a responsibility upon the parties to restrict and ultimately to abolish several forms of forced labour; in particular it prohibits the imposition of forced labour for private profit. The remaining articles set forth the steps to be taken by the Powers signatory to the Convention to bring to an end slavery in its different forms.

Sir Austen Chamberlain and Lord Cecil made a considerable effort to secure in this connection more definite obligations with regard to the trading in slaves, more particularly with a view to treating the Slave Trade as piracy. The British attitude upon this feature of the Slave Trade is set forth in one of the most courageous documents ever issued by the Foreign Office. Sir Austen Chamberlain's despatch to Sir Eric Drummond was sent in May, 1926, in the hope that the proposal would be adopted in the following September.

Sir Austen Chamberlain suggested an addition to the Convention in order to deal with slave-trading as piracy. The addition which he suggested was that Article 3 of the Convention should be amended by the insertion of the words:

> The act of conveying slaves on the high seas shall be deemed as between the high contracting parties to be the equivalent of an act of piracy and the public ships of the signatory States shall have the same rights in relation to vessels and persons engaged in such act as in relation to vessels and persons engaged in piracy.

Sir Austen Chamberlain in making this suggestion set forth very clearly the historic British position—namely, that certain crimes are regarded as being crimes against the human race and that the British Government considered that there was a general consensus of opinion in all civilised States that the Slave Trade constituted a crime of this nature. Sir Austen proceeded to declare that the British Government did not believe that at this date any civilised country would wish to challenge that opinion. It followed therefore, from the British point of view, that the slave trade by sea should be regarded as falling within the same category of crime as piracy.

There was no hesitation on the part of Sir Austen Chamberlain in making clear exactly what this would mean, and in a despatch to Sir Eric Drummond he pointed out that according to Oppenheim a pirate was considered an outlaw who would lose the protection of his home State and thereby his national character and would be considered an enemy of every State, exposed to the machinery of justice anywhere in the world. This has always meant that the pirate could be promptly hanged or drowned and his cargo confiscated.

Lord Cecil was unable to carry this proposal, owing very largely to the combined opposition of France, Italy and Portugal. All that he could do was to get incorporated in the Convention an obligation to consider the matter at a later date.

The Convention has been signed and ratified by some forty States. But it is one thing to draft, sign and ratify a Convention and it is quite another thing to get its provisions loyally carried out. The Convention had one grave defect in that no machinery was provided to watch over its practical application; moreover, as the Expert Commission pointed out, even the provision that documents relating to slavery should be forwarded to the League had never been carried out by many of the signatories—notably those in whose territories slavery in one or another of its many forms still exists over wide areas.

It was again left to Great Britain to make proposals to deal with this defect.

Lord Cecil when a member of the British Delegation at Geneva was instructed to propose that a Permanent Anti-Slavery Commission should be appointed. In the result the best that could be done was to get the matter adjourned for a year. The same thing happened in 1930. Again that great hindrance to all international progress, the spirit of nationalism, succeeded in putting off the British suggestion. However, Lord Lytton, who was the British Government's representative in 1931, succeeded in getting the Assembly to agree to the temporary re-appointment of the former Commission to enquire what progress was being made, and the British Government was able to secure the insertion of an instruction to report what changes in the machinery of the League were desirable to assist in abolishing slavery. Accordingly, the Temporary Commission resumed its sittings, and thanks to the efforts of M. Gohr and Lord Lugard, produced a most interesting report on the general question and particularly recommended the creation of a Permanent Anti-Slavery Commission of the League.

After ten years of enquiry and discussion by the League of Nations the British proposals have now been adopted. The League, by its resolution in the

Assembly of 1932, formally committed itself to the creation of machinery to bring about the 'suppression of slavery in all its forms' throughout the world.

The actual work is to be undertaken by the Secretariat of the League. The first step will be the appointment of seven expert advisers to assist the Council of the League. These are to be permanent appointments in the sense that the members will be appointed for an indefinite period, and will meet every second year. The Commission will 'cease to exist as soon as the results anticipated in the campaign against slavery had been, or were on the point of being, attained.'

The reference under which the Slavery Commission and Secretariat will work is as wide as the most ardent abolitionist could wish it to be. At the Conference of Versailles the Berlin and Brussels Acts were merged into the Treaty of St. Germain-en-Laye, and in this instrument the signatory Powers committed themselves to the 'suppression of slavery in all its forms.' Following upon the Steel-Maitland resolution of 1922, the League Council set up the Temporary Slavery Commission, part of whose duty it was to give a practical interpretation to the term 'slavery in all its forms.'

The interpretation then formulated has provided the basis of all League work since 1926. The Temporary Slavery Commission appointed in 1931 accepted the same interpretation of the reference as had been adopted by the former Slavery Commission. This interpretation has been divided into seven main categories—legal status of slaves, slave-raiding and similar acts, slave-trading, slave-dealing (including exchange, sale, gift, inheritance), practices restrictive of the liberty of the person, domestic or predial slavery, and transition from servile labour to free wage labour.

The task to which the League of Nations and, in this instance, the United States, have committed themselves is far more complex and in many ways more difficult than that which confronted Great Britain a hundred years ago. It took first Wilberforce and then Buxton forty-six years in all to bring the British Parliament to a decision, but that decision once taken (by the Act of 1833) Emancipation came into force only one year later. It has taken only ten years to bring the League of Nations to agree to attempt world abolition and emancipation, but he would be a bold man who would predict how many years it will take to carry through the programme envisaged by the League of Nations.

Sir John Simon has recently said of the League decision :

> To-day a new and greater Parliament of the world is trying to make the new international spirit the effective motive force for world reform. Can it do on the greater stage of the world something which corresponds to what was done in our own national life by Wilberforce and his friends ? It will be an immense achievement and the most significant indication of the reality of this new international world order. It is in the nature of things an infinitely more difficult task than our national task ever was, because what was done 100 years ago was done after a crusade of a generation. It had the law behind it and therefore there was a considerable prospect of making it effective. The difficulty at Geneva is that general resolutions and aspirations, which I will not call pious, are so much more difficult to make effective. One of the great tests of the usefulness of Geneva will be whether the nations

will or will not be able to see something real done in the next few years for the abolition of slavery from the world.

This was no idle warning by Sir John Simon. Whether or not the League will respond effectively to his challenge will depend upon two factors: public opinion in all countries and moral leadership at Geneva.

The League is a great institution, the one good thing which has emerged from the miseries of the Great War. But if there had been no Nansen, no Gohr, and above all, no Cecil, it is more than doubtful whether the League would have set itself the task of abolishing slavery throughout the world.

After a struggle lasting over a hundred years the nations of the world now possess an international treaty and an international instrument equipped for the great task of securing the total abolition of slavery in all its forms. But the machine can only function at its full capacity if it is sustained by an international conscience, vocal in every country attached to the League of Nations. Lady Simon spoke no truer word than when she proclaimed :

> The fight calls for all our energies, and there is but one weapon to hand. That weapon is Public Opinion—at once the weakest and the strongest weapon in the cause of human progress : weak when dormant, but invincible when once roused to the pitch of zealous indignation.

The official organ of the League of Nations—*i.e.* the Expert Committee on Slavery—is also emphatic as to the essential services of public opinion, for in recommending the creation of permanent machinery their Report states that 'the mere existence of such a Commission would enlighten world public opinion as to the position in regard to slavery in the world, and would foster the growth of a movement of opinion which must be expected to produce favourable results for the disappearance of slavery in all its forms.'

In the section covering 'suggestions' for the abolition of slavery the League Committee again places in the forefront the value of public opinion:

it is certain that, if public opinion in all countries paid constant attention to the slavery question, the Abyssinian people would realise that no country can be regarded as fully civilized while it continues to tolerate slavery.

Hundreds of thousands of freed slaves alive and happy at this very moment owe their liberty to present-day public opinion. It is often overlooked that nearly 500,000 slaves have been set free within the last twenty years—and set free by public opinion.

The Maharajah of Nepal, in his great Emancipation Speech of 1924 at Khatmandu, supported his eloquent plea for the liberation of slaves by a powerful array of figures, incidents and arguments, and amongst the latter he used that of public opinion. 'The enlightened opinion of the civilized world with whom we are coming into more intimate contact now, is pressing on us with all its moral force'—and 58,000 slaves were set free.

In the Sierra Leone Protectorate there had existed in slavery more than 200,000 slaves for generations; the lack of public opinion was responsible for its continuance, for without it the Governor could not secure abolition. Sir Ransford Slater, always anxious to abolish slavery, said in one of his reports: 'there is a total absence of any "public opinion" in Sierra Leone adverse to the system. Churches and Missions abound in Sierra Leone, but I have received no word from them on the subject, nor can I find any record of any representation from them to any of my predecessors.'[1]

The startling incident which shook public opinion out of its lethargy arose from an Appeal Case in Sierra Leone. Two slaves in the Protectorate had run away, had been pursued and retaken by their masters, who in turn were prosecuted for assault and defended themselves on the ground that they had merely exercised a reasonable degree of force to recover their *property*, and that since slavery was legal in the Protectorate of Sierra Leone they were justified in recapturing their property.

The Judges of the Supreme Court were Mr. Justice Petrides, Mr. Justice Sawrey-Cookson and Mr. Justice Aitken, who by a majority of two to one upheld the case of the masters. The essential passages in the long judgment pronounced by Mr. Justice Sawrey-Cookson are: 'Here then we have the clearest possible recognition of a slave who is owned much as a chattel can be owned, and it must logically result that there is a right to follow and regain by use of any lawful means the rights of ownership in and possession of the property of which he has been deprived by the absconding of his slave . . . until the Legislature makes it perfectly clear that no such right to retake is to be recognised, I cannot find that the law as it stands at present denied that right to the slave-owner in the Protectorate.'

The arrival in England of the full text of the judgment created consternation in the Press and in the

[1] Sessional Paper No. 5 of 1926.

legal world. Sir John Simon drew public attention to the judgment in a letter to *The Times*, and *The Times*, the *Manchester Guardian* and most of the daily papers of the United Kingdom published the judgment almost in full. Whilst successive Secretaries of State had for years known of the situation in the Protectorate and had made some feeble attempts to reform it, nothing effectual was done until the Press had created the impelling force of public opinion.

To Mr. Amery belongs the credit for having at once taken vigorous action. He informed the Governor that it was impossible for him as Colonial Secretary to defend the position in Sierra Leone, and a few days later advised the Governor to call a special session of the Legislature in order that legislation might be passed rapidly through the local council—and 214,000 slaves were set free in Sierra Leone Protectorate on January 1, 1924.

Sir Harcourt Butler was the Emancipator of the slaves in Burma, but again it was only possible for him to carry through the work because public opinion was behind him.

In the memorandum, dated August 7, 1928, submitted to Sir Eric Drummond for the information of the League of Nations, Sir Harcourt Butler was able to report that slavery had practically ceased to exist in Burma. Thus slavery was ended on the Eastern side of India, while on the Western side the Government of India was able to report to the League of Nations its final abolition in Baluchistan, where, in 1926, a decree was signed that from November 4 of that year private property in slaves had ceased to exist—and nearly another 9,000 slaves were set free.

Before the War there were 185,000 slaves in the German Territory of East Africa, and on March 19, 1914, an attempt was made in the German Reichstag to secure the emancipation of these slaves by January, 1920. Unfortunately, public opinion had not been sufficiently aroused to justify the Government in accepting the resolution, and the proposal was dropped when it was pointed out that it would involve the payment of nearly half a million of money in 1915 and a second payment of more than a quarter of a million in 1920. At the end of the War, as a result of the Conference at Versailles, and the undertaking of the nations to bring about the total abolition of slavery, the whole of the slaves were set free throughout German East Africa, now a British Mandated Territory under the name of Tanganyika.

The question asked by Sir John Simon on page 230 as to whether or not the League will be able to secure the complete abolition of slavery can only be answered by public opinion. If the public of 1933–34 and onwards is less determined than in 1833–34, then the League will fail in its attempt, but if a real international conscience can be brought into active being, then the League will succeed in its task of setting free the slaves of the world.

CHAPTER XV

Slavery To-day

What is Slavery?—5,000,000 Slaves—Serfdom—The Price of Women—Tortures—Slave-breeding—The Mekka Slave Market—Slavery in China—Slave-raiding—Captain Yardley—Herr Grühl—Sir Arnold Hodson.

What is Slavery? In practice it means three great evils: Slave-owning, Slave-raiding and Slave-trading, altogether apart from analogous systems such as Forced Labour for private profit and certain forms of Contract Labour. Slave-owning is the root of the whole matter, and Emancipators and Abolitionists alike have for many years realised that until that institution is abolished the demand for slaves will persist and the 'goods' will be provided by slave-trading or slave-raiding. On the evidence available ten years ago, it was estimated that there were 3,000,000 slaves in the world, but on the more extensive evidence now available we know that the former estimate was too low and that the total must exceed 5,000,000.

What is a slave? Until 1925 definitions of slavery reposed upon national legislative enactments or legal opinions. The Anti-Slavery Convention of 1926 for the first time gave a definition accepted by all States Members of the League of Nations: 'Slavery is a status or condition of a person over whom any or all the powers attaching to the right of ownership are exercised.' That is, a slave is just a property. The slave thus has no human rights, no rights of speech, no rights of conscience, no rights of property because he or she is a property. The slave has no domestic rights, both wife and husband are a saleable asset, mother and daughter, father and son can have no personal association except at the will of the owner. Parents can be sold away from children, sons and daughters can be sold from parents. Neither their labour nor their persons are their own, they are entitled to no wages and their necessary sustenance is at the arbitrary will of their owner. Finally, their punishments, whether of whip, stock, branding irons or mutilations, are decided and inflicted not by Courts of Justice but subject to the uncontrolled will of the owner of the property.

The figure of 5,000,000 is sometimes challenged because it is not based upon any census. The figure is, it is true, only an estimate, but it rests upon information supplied by persons of authority in most territories. Take first that of China. The most precise figure is that given by Mr. Coates in his book on China,[1] in which he states that 2,000,000 is a 'very moderate estimate.' That the total is a large one is confirmed by a report from Mr. Russell Brown, the British Consul in Amoy, and published in an official White Paper[2]: 'Girls are everywhere bought and sold for maid servants or slaves.' The probability is that the total number of slave girls held as a property amongst the 400,000,000 Chinese in China, Mongolia and the outer territories is considerably in excess of the estimate of 2,000,000.

[1] C. H. Coates, *The Red Theology in the Far East.*

[2] Cmd. 3424.

As a slave-owning country on a large scale, Abyssinia apparently comes next to China. The *Morning Post* of January 9, 1926, published an anonymous article by a writer of exceptional authority and experience who estimated that there were at least 2,000,000 slaves in Abyssinia. Another estimate, made by the official of a European Government, is that 'one-fifth of the people of Abyssinia are slaves.' If the total population of Abyssinia is 10,000,000, one-fifth gives again the figure of 2,000,000. A third authority is a British official, Captain Cochrane, who has lived many years on the frontier of Abyssinia. In a letter which is incorporated in a Foreign Office paper he states: 'I will say practically every (but think every) Abyssinian on the frontier has a slave or slaves.' This letter shows how widespread is the system imposed upon the subject races and lower orders by the 4,000,000 Abyssinians of the ruling races and classes. An American writer tells us that some of the Rases or petty kings own as many as 15,000 slaves each. The Emperor of Abyssinia is doing his best, in face of great difficulties, to abolish slavery and has undertaken to do so within twenty years. He is understood to contest the popular estimate of 2,000,000, being of the opinion that the total number of slaves to-day is considerably less than 1,000,000. The only satisfactory method of establishing a correct figure would be to take a census of the slaves.

Exact estimates of slaves in other areas are unobtainable. The population of Arabia is estimated at 7,000,000, and if the proportion of slaves to free people is approximately that of Abyssinia, say one-fifth, there would be 1,400,000 slaves—it is probable that half that number, 700,000, would be a modest estimate.

These estimates give for China, Arabia, Abyssinia, 4,700,000, but that figure leaves out altogether Liberia and certain other areas where slave-owning in one or other of its many forms is known to be deeply rooted in the customs of the country. Thus 5,000,000 appears to be below the actual number of men, women and children held to-day as a property in violation of the Anti-Slavery Convention of 1926.

The systems of slave-owning are indeed numerous, moreover there are several institutions which if they do not cross the borderline come perilously near to it. First come systems of admitted slavery—that is, where ownership is clearly and frankly recognised, as in Abyssinia and Arabia.

Next come those like the 'Adoption' or Mui Tsai systems of China or Hong Kong. There is no question in the minds of any impartial persons that the word 'Adoption,' to quote Mr. Russell Brown, is a mere 'euphemism.' The fact that the girls are called slaves, figure in public documents as slaves, are bought and sold in the market and street as slaves, shatters the flimsy contention of interested apologists. The Editor of the *Hong Kong Daily Press* has no doubt as to the position of a Mui Tsai: 'There is no disguising the fact that a Mui Tsai is a slave. She is transferred from her natural parents to another family on payment of money, and becomes the property of her purchaser.'

During a debate in the House of Commons on May 11, 1931, Sir John Simon greatly impressed members by producing the actual bill of sale of a Mui Tsai. He said: 'I think I can show the Committee that these little girls are frequently the subject of a bill of sale just as the negro slaves were subject to bills of sale in the eighteenth century in the West Indies and the Southern States of America. I have here both the original and the translation of such a bill of sale.' Sir John Simon concluded his forceful speech by appealing to heads of families in the House:

> If there is any Member now sitting in this Committee who has in his own family a child of that age or a grandchild he will know why some people condemn such an adoption as this. She is sold through the intermediary of an agent, whose name is given—Ho Kwai Tse—to a woman, whose name is given, residing at a particular address in Hong Kong.

The Abyssinian system of slavery is no less widespread and no less difficult to eradicate than those of China and Mongolia. As Lord Noel-Buxton pointed out after his recent visit to Abyssinia, slavery is fundamental to the whole economic and ecclesiastical system of the country. It is probably true that here again many of the slaves are fairly well treated, but that large numbers are the victims of cruelty cannot be doubted. Herr Grühl in his book [1] on recent travels in Abyssinia has some pitifully eloquent passages upon what slavery really means.

Herr Grühl says that during his purely scientific studies he often put questions to slaves, the answers to which 'brought before my eyes human tragedies that even the most powerful imagination could scarcely have conceived.' He describes a conversation with what appeared to be a very old woman, whose 'bent back told its own tale and whose furrowed and wrinkled face spoke of a care-filled life.' Instead of her apparent sixty years Herr Grühl calculated that she was only

[1] Max Grühl, *The Citadel of Ethiopia.*

between thirty and forty years old. This woman slave had been sold from place to place on the way from Lake Rudolf; she had produced many children by different owners.

She could only tell me about two of her children; she knew nothing of the others. She had borne two children to her owner in X, one to another owner in Y, one to the servant of this man, and one to a man who had been staying with her owner in Z, and so on. Long scars showed on her thighs and back—the marks made by a 'chiraf' or whip. On the upper part of her right arm and on her breasts were round scars left by branding-irons. The slaves are burnt with red-hot irons in this fashion in order to 'increase their strength.' At present this 'old' woman of thirty to forty is employed in grinding meal for the servant of her owner. A few more years—and she will disappear, worn-out, a piece of human refuse. . . .

That is what slavery means to-day! Apart from its inhuman cruelty, there is the degradation and demoralisation which always accompanies it and constitutes one of its most repellent features.

The slave-owning systems of Mohammedan Arabia are almost identical with those of Christian Abyssinia. There is probably no greater authority upon the situation in and around Mekka than Mr. Eldon Rutter, who has described the situation in Arabia very fully in his book.[1] Mr. Rutter, writing to the author a few months ago, said that 'Slavery exists in every part of Arabia with the exception of Aden as a normal social institution, but I have seen only one actual slave market where slaves are displayed for sale in a public place like merchandise. This was in Mekka.'

But alas, this does not complete the sorry tale of

[1] Eldon Rutter, *The Holy Cities of Arabia.*

slave-owning, for beyond the bounds of the estimated 5,000,000 there are the unknown numbers in bondage under 'analogous systems.' First amongst these is peonage, the system which in Putumayo led to individual atrocities more revolting than under any other slave system known to recorded history. The Slavery Commission which the League of Nations set up in 1925 drew attention to the very large areas in South America in which peonage prevails and quoted a recent authoritative statement as follows: 'The peonage system is one of the exacting problems that South American nations must face.' The statement goes on to describe how the peon is 'constantly in debt to his overlord. This debt hanging over him reduces him to practical slavery . . . the peon is tied to the land . . . in selling the property the peons pass to the new owner. Theoretically free, they are practically unable to break away from their yoke.' The organ of the Italian Anti-Slavery Society [1] has recently published some interesting material upon the system as it is working to-day in certain parts of Central and South America, and the writer thus sums up the main features of the system:

> It is impossible to give numerical statistics, but they are numbered in their thousands. In Ilanos of Venezuela each big farm or plantation has often over a thousand of them and in general each farm has some thirty of these families—slaves in all but name. . . . They are the property of their master, who does with them what he wishes without any control. These slaves rarely have recourse to the authorities, of whom they more often than not ignore the existence,

[1] *Journal of the Italian Anti-Slavery Society*, August and September, 1932.

and to approach whom they lack the means. They receive no religious instruction, and no education. They exist, that is all. Work, suffering, illness, drunkenness sometimes, and death are the landmarks of their lives.

The system under which these peons are held is the usual one. As the writer says :

They are shown in figures the debts they have contracted for dress and food, and are thus prevented from returning to their homes. If they attempt escape they are imprisoned or severely punished. Prisons are always provided in these big farms and properties. If they manage to escape, the police generally favour their proprietors and bring the fugitives back in chains.

Another 'analogous system' is that of pledging. This obtains in several African territories and probably reached its largest and most deplorable dimensions in Liberia, but it seems very doubtful whether the system there can be abolished or even controlled until something has been done to provide the country with a civilised government capable of keeping order and administering justice.

The situation in Liberia became such a gross international scandal that it was brought to the notice of the League of Nations, and so strong was the pressure of world public opinion that in very shame the Liberian representative himself invited enquiry. A small International Commission, which included Mr. Edwin Barclay, Ex-President of Liberia, Dr. Johnson of the U.S.A., and Dr. Christy, was appointed, and its Report, issued in 1931, not only confirmed the allegations that had been made, but brought to light a state of affairs so serious that, in the emphatic words used by Viscount Snowden in the House of Lords on

March 16, 1932, 'the revelations of that Report shocked the moral conscience of the whole world.'

The evidence showed that 2,000,000 natives were suffering oppression and cruelty at the hands of the 15,000 Americo-Liberians and that in the words of a Washington despatch, 'the twin scourges of slavery and forced labour' existed on a large scale. This report shattered the complacency of the defenders of the Liberian Government, whilst their discomfiture was still more complete when the Government itself formally accepted as true the findings of the Commission. One of the charges confirmed was the existence of a system of servitude known as pawning, which in Liberia had become barely distinguishable from slave-owning. A native once pawned could not be redeemed except by a third party—that is, it was made impossible for the person pawned to redeem himself or herself. The local price of a pawn was the local price of a slave. The Commission illustrated this system by quoting several instances, in some of which the Government was clearly involved. A headman near Royesville was fined £18 for failure to attend to the roads, but he could only pay the Government by pawning his wife and child, who had been in pawn five years when the Commission arrived in Liberia; another man was fined £17, in order to pay which he had to pawn his sons, who after two years in pawn still saw no prospect of redemption. Another man was compelled to pawn his son, but as the son ran away, the court increased the fines, which automatically increased the amount for which the boy was held. It was not merely the ordinary natives of Liberia who engaged in the practice, for the Commission stated that the President himself was a party to one such incident, when he fined a chief £20, a sum which the latter could only pay by pawning his child.

The third 'analogous system' is serfdom, and the line which divides serfdom from slavery is so exceedingly fine as to be scarcely perceptible. In Hyderabad, for example, a system has been disclosed in a report issued by Mr. S. K. Iyengar, who was appointed a special investigation officer. This officer undertook an enquiry into the systems of serfdom obtaining in Hyderabad, and selected for this purpose twelve villages. Mr. Iyengar divides the system of serfdom into a twofold category: the bhagela and the jattipani. In one of these systems Mr. Iyengar says that no wages are paid to the workers and if they refuse they are whipped and then dragged to the fields. In one village in which the investigation was made the rights exercised by the masters over the serfs are absolute.

In Abyssinia also there appears to be a system of serfdom running parallel with slavery. Monsieur Angoulvant, formerly Governor of French West Africa, later of French Equatorial Africa and a member of the League of Nations Slavery Commission, expressed the view that side by side with slavery in Abyssinia exists a system of domestic serfdom.

At the same time there are forms of serfdom which cannot be said to amount to property ownership of persons, for, as the Temporary Commission on Slavery said in its Report to the Council of the League, 'There is no doubt that, in addition to slavery proper, which admits the traditional conception of a master's ownership of a human being, serfdom also exists under which this conception is excluded altogether, since the serf, if he remains with his master, does so of his own free will.'

Finally, there is the very large category of women who are obtained for various purposes by means of purchase disguised as dowry. Let it be admitted, as it must be, that this practice is largely a social custom and that it has good elements in it; let it also be admitted that the natives draw a line between free women obtained by dowry and women purchased as slaves. When all this and much more has been said it cannot be claimed that the system is one which should be perpetuated or that abuses of a most serious kind are not often committed.

The Temporary Slavery Commission of the League, which included one woman, were apparently unanimous in the view that native marriage customs have given rise to abuses which in some cases have involved a regular trade in wives. They were unable to regard the well-known 'lobolo'[1] system as a form of slavery, but they held that the system of concubinage in certain territories is, on the other hand, much more likely to lead to traffic in slaves, since the acquisition of a concubine is usually accompanied by the payment of a certain sum which constitutes a real sale of the woman.

The treatment of these millions of slaves varies widely; it is probably true that the majority are well

[1] The 'lobolo' system may be defined as follows. A man obtains his wife by a payment of cattle or goods. This payment may take him many years and has the advantage of forming a kind of insurance for good treatment. On the other hand, it is becoming a system not only of selling, but even of leasing wives on the part of the chiefs and is now resulting in grave abuses.

treated, but as Professor Forster, an eye-witness of Chinese slavery, says :

> The sale of the girl by the parents is in itself such a shock to the child's self-respect, that it utterly destroys forever that feeling of individual worthwhileness and self-confidence. The foundation on which the child's personality is to be reared is thus swept away. The stimulus to moral and spiritual growth having been subtracted, the whole development of the child as a human being is arrested.

A missionary in China who is unwilling that her name should be published writes upon the question of treatment in a manner which is probably as fair a statement as can well be made :

> In some cases the girls are well and sufficiently clothed and fed, and treated well, but from what I have seen, or from inquiries made of Chinese, I fear that most slave girls are very hardly and very often cruelly treated. I have personally come across cases of unimaginable cruelty, which I am told are by no means isolated instances.

The plain psychological fact is that the ownership of one person by another too often excites the worst passions, more particularly when the wishes and desires of the owner are thwarted. The potential brutality of ownership is sometimes equally apparent in the treatment of a horse or a dog. Shakespeare's understanding of the mentality of ownership is shown by the words which he puts into the mouth of Shylock :

> What judgment shall I dread, doing no wrong ?
> You have among you many a purchased slave,
> Which like your asses and your dogs and mules,
> You use in abject and in slavish parts,
> Because you bought them.

Authenticated instances of present-day barbarities

inflicted on slaves leave little or nothing lacking in refinements of torture. In China there are constant reports of branding the slaves with hot irons, the well-known torture of amputating joints of fingers and toes, the boiling water and the boiling oil punishment, the hanging up by hands and thumbs—indeed, as one surveys the mass of reports upon the treatment of the child slaves of China, it is doubtful whether the misery and degradation of the mass and the acute agonies of many are surpassed under any system of slavery in the world. We know but little of the cruelties inflicted upon the slaves of Arabia and the Persian Gulf, but Dr. Harrison, a missionary of some fourteen years' experience, tells us that these are of such a terrible nature that the mere thought of the punishment to be inflicted will almost cause the victim to lose his reason :

> When one of these negro slaves starts up as if suddenly crazed and runs round shouting and gesticulating and talking earnestly in a changed voice as if a new personality had possessed him even the hard Arab masters are a good deal awed and hesitate to inflict the punishment they had planned.[1]

The same conditions apply to Abyssinia. Lord Noel-Buxton tells us in his report that 'slavery is fundamental to the whole economic system of Abyssinia, that the majority of slaves render domestic services and are not usually put to hard work, some of them are even treated as members of the family.' On the other hand, M. Kessel, a French traveller who visited Abyssinia in 1930, has told how while he sat at dinner with a young Abyssinian noble (who had been brought

[1] Dr. Harrison, *The Arab at Home.*

up by French priests) pitiful cries of a child were heard, which were explained by the host as coming from a little boy slave (belonging to a neighbour) who was tied up for 'correction.' The host sent a slave with a message to say that his guests were disturbed—more blows were heard, then silence. Kessel discovered later that while they sat at dinner the child had died under the strokes of the sjambok (whip). Reliable witnesses say that in the remoter regions the slaves are subjected to the chain, the lash, the stocks, and in the case of baby boys gelding in order to increase their market value.

There are still those who defend slavery as an institution. They are unable to plumb the depths of suffering into which these millions of helpless people are plunged by the degrading influence of slavery upon the owner. It is true that they become occasionally indignant at reports of cruel and atrocious suffering inflicted upon particular slaves, but they quiet their misgivings with the hope that such cruelties are exceptional. Their mentality with regard to slave-trading and slave-raiding is different. These proceedings arouse immediate indignation, but the tragedy is that people do not see that slave-raiding and slave-trading will only come to an end with the suppression of slave-owning, or, stated quite crudely, that it is only when the market has been abolished that the supply will cease.

The story of supplying the market has been and still is being written in the blood and tears of its victims. The recruiter, the raider, the trader are each of them to-day playing their dreadful parts in this unholy traffic, they ply their instruments of torture as of old; the whip, the stock, the branding irons, chains and yokes, the cutlass and the gun. Let there be no delusion, these agents and their instruments are just as necessary to the institution of slavery as a slaughter-house is to slaughter.

There is not a single law of the decalogue which is not broken daily in order to supply the market; envy, hatred, avarice and malice, outrage and murder, are the normal accompaniments of the trade. It is an institution run for profit, and 'the love of money is the root of all evil.' To-day more than at any previous period in history we are citizens of the world family, and it is surely the duty of every man and woman to examine with firm courage the cruel lot of so many fellow members of that world family. Too often their sufferings are hidden, but sometimes it is possible to lift the curtain far enough to get an insight into some of the incidentals of slavery.

It may be true that slave-breeding—however degrading it may be—involves in its early stages the least amount of cruelty, but it presupposes entire lack of respect for human personality. The practice is now believed to be limited to some three or four areas, but no area where slave-owning obtains can be regarded as immune. The rearing of slaves was one of the revolting accompaniments of slavery that stirred the late Maharajah of Nepal to action. But in denouncing the practice he was careful to base his plea for its abolition on practical as well as moral grounds. In his emancipation speech he devoted one section to what he called the 'inhuman practice' of breeding child slaves, and declared this to be the worst feature of the institution of slavery. Facing the masters in the audience he asked them whether they really thought this practice brought any gain to them, and he invited their attention to a set of figures which he had prepared for their information. He took as his basic figure a woman bearing six children and pointed out that each child would only fetch 35 rupees, a figure which he stated was far below what the owner could earn by other methods of investment.

The Maharajah stated that it had been contended that better prices could be obtained for certain children. In reply to this objection he said, 'Those who say that they get better prices at prevailing rates should remember that a woman of child-bearing age would also cost more than the legal price, and that the larger sum and the other expenses, if invested as in the "appendix," would have brought them sums which it is very difficult for them to obtain by sale of children. Again, the woman may die, or may turn out to be barren, or less prolific—and as infant mortality is so heavy here, the child also may die before attaining a saleable age. These probabilities discount greatly the expectations built by the masters.' The Maharajah concluded that 'slave rearing then, either for labour or for sale, is not the profitable business you believe it to be.'

A kindred practice and, according to the Maharajah of Nepal, an equally reprehensible one, was prevalent in order to supply the slave markets. Under this practice the slave-owners were accustomed to give slave girls to share the bed of men who were too poor and needy to sustain any claim over the children, and thus the child became the property of the owner. As the Maharajah said, 'it is by such demoralizing ways that slaves can be bred for the market bringing an apparent profit to the master of the girl,' and he concluded :

> If selling slave children, parting them from their mothers at a tender age, is reprehensible, this way of breeding them is more so. It would not surprise us, after this, to be told that if disappointed with one man in the number of children begotten, the master in some cases compels the girl to share the bed of another just as a breeder does with his cattle and lets one bull after another serve a cow.

In 1930 the Editor of *Le Matin* organised and despatched to Abyssinia, the Red Sea and Arabia, a highly competent Commission of Enquiry. The leader of this Commission was M. Kessel. Other members of the Commission were Lieut. Lablache-Combier and Dr. Emile Peyre. M. Kessel, in one of the twenty articles published in *Le Matin* describing the work of the Commission, dealt with the question of supplying the slave market with slaves. Dealing particularly with the Hedjaz, he stated that the supply of human merchandise is kept up in two ways: the first of these is that of 'breeding for the market,' and the second the overseas trade. With regard to the first he declared that 'There are organised means at work to multiply the offspring; there even exists a corps of female agents who keep in touch with the owners on the control of reproduction on the selective principle, and are rewarded when a child is born.'

M. Marcel Griaule, a French scientific investigator, went out to Abyssinia apparently with no idea of studying the question of slavery, but it was thrust upon his attention wherever he went. In one part of his report, which was issued by the International Labour Office of the League of Nations, he also deals with the question of slave production for the market and states that :

The slave is utilised at the will of his master in any and every department of ordinary life, including reproduction in the case of a woman. In fact, just as live stock is placed in favourable conditions for breeding, so a male may be assigned to a female slave in order that their offsprings may add to their owner's property. It is however more usual to let these people form ties as they will, so long as it does not interfere with their work; moreover they can be separated at any time just as may suit their owners. A woman slave may not take advantage of her pregnancy to stop her work for a time. She continues her work until the actual day of her delivery and resumes it almost immediately afterwards. Only the desire of the master not to depreciate his goods by demanding exertions which might injure the mother's health and lessen the value of the child ever softens the rigours of this custom.

We are sometimes told that children are born free in Abyssinia ; this may be so in certain provinces, but according to M. Griaule it is certainly not the case with children bred for the market, for as he says :

the child belongs to the owner of the mother at the day of birth, even if the father is a free man ; a free father has the right to buy his child's freedom. . . . The owner has theoretically the right to dispose of the child from the moment of its birth ; he can take the baby from the breast and sell it. As a matter of fact, it is clear that the owner's interests demand that the new-born child should live under the best possible conditions, so that he may be a fine specimen if sold young or that he may develop normally and become a vigorous worker. These two reasons usually prevail to prevent the child being taken from his mother until he is weaned.

In Arabia there is a variant of this practice. Mr. Eldon Rutter says that there are numbers of very poor foreigners in Arabia who are unable to find the necessary means to procure and liberate a wife; these are able to obtain women upon the agreed basis that any child they 'produce,' being born into slavery, is handed over to the owner of the woman as a property to be disposed of by him in the markets. The breeding of slaves is a revolting practice, degrading to the women purchased for breeding purposes. It may break the hearts of the mothers to have their little children torn from them and their baby boys mutilated prior to sale in the market, but it is in trading and raiding that the more brutal atrocities are committed. There are some recognised markets for slaves, but the vast majority are sold by private dealers. In certain cities in China agents stand in the streets with children for sale—a straw plait indicating that the child awaits a purchaser.

Let us look at one slave market as described by Mr. Eldon Rutter in a letter to the author:

> The slave market in Mekka is a street leading to one of the gates of the Great Mosque. At certain hours of the day male and female slaves are made to sit on stone benches in front of the houses, so that the passers-by may inspect them. They are dressed in the gown worn by the poorer natives of the city, and the faces of the women are veiled. They lift their veils if requested to do so. Any closer inspection of a slave by a prospective purchaser takes place inside the slave-dealer's house. Young women at that time realised the equivalent of £60 to £70 each, according to youth, beauty, and efficiency in household duties. Male slaves were slightly less expensive.

But even in Mekka the open slave market is not the principal channel of the trade, for according to Mr. Rutter, in most towns other than Mekka 'the slaves are sold privately. In some places there are dealers who keep a definite stock of slaves ; in others there are merely agents who dispose of any slave whom a private person may desire to sell.'

In the Holy Cities of Arabia, Mr. Eldon Rutter recounts an extremely interesting conversation which he had with an eminent Mohammedan. This conversation confirms in several interesting particulars M. Kessel's evidence on the methods of supplying the slave markets of Arabia :

'Had I but two hundred or three hundred guineas,' said Shafîg, between the whiffs of his shîsha, 'I could profit much from slaves. I know a place of slaves.'

'Where is that ?' I enquired.

'Above from El Gunfuda,' he replied, 'on the coast of the sea between Birk and El Hodayda, to the south.'

I was sitting with the cronies in Abdurrahmân's mag'od. It was near the hour of the midday prayer, and without the iron-barred window the narrow lane was vivid with burning sunlight. But in this bottom room of the tall house the air was cool and dank. A dingy air-shaft, a foot in width, ran up to the roof, and iron gratings opened into it on every landing of the dark stairway.

'And those slaves—are they Yemenîs or Habashîs ?'[1] asked Abdul Fattâh.

'Yemenîs,' replied Shafîg. 'They are said to be children stolen from their parents in the inner wilderness of the Yemen. And Allah is More Knowing. There are Habashîs also.'

'But when they bring the Habashîs from Africa, O my uncle,' I said, 'do they land them at El Gunfuda ?'

'No,' said he, 'they land them more to southward near El Hodayda ; for there the distance between Arabia and Africa is not great. Their desire is to pass the sea quickly.''

'They say that some of the people of the Yemen sell their own children,' said Hasan.

[1] Abyssinians.

'I take refuge in God,' exclaimed Shafîg. 'But there are people who own men-slaves and women-slaves ; so they let them breed, in order that they may profit by selling the children !'

The actual marketing of slaves is probably carried on to a greater extent in China than elsewhere. It was the late Archbishop of Canterbury who first drew public attention to this during a debate in the House of Lords. Dr. Davidson recounted a conversation which had just taken place between an eminent Chinaman and himself. He stated that in conversation he himself drew a very dark picture of the state of China as it appeared to him, and said that the picture seemed so dark that he hardly liked to put it to this eminent Chinaman as being true, but emphasised that he was speaking of Western China where slavery is rife, but he presumed that it was not possible to purchase slaves in the great cities of the East. His Chinese friend replied 'Oh, yes, it is. I could buy them in half an hour. There is not the slightest difficulty in buying girls ; I could buy them anywhere.'

In 1930 an appeal was issued in Europe, signed jointly by leading Chinese and well-known missionaries in China. This appeal was published for the purpose of securing funds to create Homes for Freed Slaves in China. In this appeal it was asserted that

last month a Missionary coming from an inland city saw little girls carried on the backs of men who were driving pack-horses ; they were being bargained for at different stopping places. In ordinary times little girls are brought to the cities, and even into other provinces, and sold by the hundreds, but in times of famine or calamity by the thousands.

Mrs. Dymond, a missionary of forty years' experience in China, states in her book[1] that 'during the terrible famine in her province 4,000 little girls were carried pack-saddle twelve days' journey to the capital city and sold.'

The principal overseas markets to-day are along the coasts of the Red Sea. This traffic takes two main forms—first, the transport and sale of slaves by Arab slave dhows; secondly—and this is probably more extensive—the inclusion in the retinues of Pilgrims to the Holy City of Mekka, of natives of Africa and the Far East for sale. The Commission of the League of Nations has drawn attention to this traffic and to the fact that it includes a feature hitherto unsuspected—namely, that this is a traffic not merely from the Continent of Africa but also from the Far East, carried on by the Mohammedan Pilgrims. Lady Simon, in her admirable book on slavery, quotes the statement of a British Naval Officer, Commander Woodward, that the total Red Sea traffic is not less than 5,000 men, women and children each year.

In the Kessel articles published in *Le Matin* it was pointed out that the importation is of a two-fold nature, the Pilgrim traffic and the ordinary Red Sea traffic. The Commission sent by *Le Matin* reported upon this dual traffic as follows:

> The pilgrim method of which the Scotch captain spoke and which was confirmed at Djeddah is less dangerous. The slaves are embarked well within all the regulations as pilgrims, but they never return. Then it also comes about that parents who have taken their whole family to the Sacred City are beggared by the exploitation of faith practised there, and sell their children in order to have money with which to return . . .

[1] *Yunnan.*

the fact that men are bought and sold, when once the threshold of the Red Sea is passed, is not realised by those who cross it in the great liners full of comfort, pleasure and music. As for an ordinary merchandise dominated by the law of supply and demand, there is for the slave trade the region where raw material is found, exporters, intermediaries, consumers on the spot and outside. There are variable prices according to the abundance of the supply and the difficulties of transport.

While slave-owning is degrading and slave-marketing is both degrading and cruel, slave-raiding gathers to itself every form of bestiality, every form of atrocious cruelty, spreading terror far and wide over the areas raided and carrying with it fire and sword, bloodshed and death to the bravest of the men as well as to the women and children, sick and afflicted. The most authoritative description to-day of a modern slave raid is to be found in the written statement of the present Governor of Sierra Leone, Sir Arnold Hodson, who had previously spent many years in an official capacity in East Africa. His vivid description should stir to generous activity all those who value human life :

> The method of raiding is to surround a village in the dark, the raiders blowing trumpets and uttering bloodthirsty yells to stampede the inhabitants. The huts are then fired, and the old men and women are ruthlessly speared or shot down as they rush out panic-stricken, only the younger ones being of sufficient value to capture.[1]

Captain Yardley, another British official, who has been an eye-witness of these raids, emphasises the well-known fact that whilst most of the raids in Abyssinia are between kingdom and kingdom, many of the raiders carry their depredations into British administered territories. Captain Yardley in his book

[1] Sir Arnold Hodson, *Where Lion Reign.*

'Parergon,' which contains an interesting preface by Field Marshal Lord Allenby, says:

> Of late years we have shirked responsibilities which are essentially our own. Free born people, men, women, and children, who are virtually our subjects, and who should look to us for protection, have been seized in their native villages from under our very noses, and carried off to lives of slavery. The soldiery of southern Abyssinia have been implicated in these expeditions in search of our people for more years than it is pleasant to count. Rape is part of the women's share of the misery. Their children have been taken from them, their menfolk mutilated, and their villages plundered by the troops of a so-called friendly State.

The number of raids into British administered territories is mounting up to a formidable figure. The officially recorded raids of recent years are now nearing a total of 200. The raiders are usually well-armed bands and generally employ anything up to a thousand rifles. It is true that the main object of these raids is often ivory and cattle, but the raiders with the blood lust upon them will murder or capture all who cross their pathway, and whatever will sell is carried off, whether it be ivory tusks, oxen, women or children.

Captain Yardley in a burst of indignant protest exclaims in his book:

> If the Imperial Government of Ethiopia cannot prevent these raids, invasions and seizure of human beings from territory which belongs to us, and not to them, the simplest remedy is for us to stop it. . . .
>
> The victims are the murdered men and women, stolen children, outraged women, mutilated men, and whole tribes and families dispossessed of their stock and personal belongings. That they should look towards our people for redress of their wrongs, and protection in the future, is perfectly reasonable and right.

Sir Arnold Hodson in his book [1] describes in considerable detail what actually happens during these raids. After surrounding a village the people are rounded up and the older men and women who are useless for the market are put to death, and he tells us that during his travels he met numbers of eye-witnesses of these raids who depicted to him the horrors they have seen:

> Enormous gangs of men, women and children have been taken from their particular villages and exposed to all the hardships of long treks through the wet and cold country, some of them in chains, and with very little food and no clothes, and when sick or exhausted they have been left to die on the road.

The chief difficulty in Abyssinia is that almost every king under the sovereignty of the King of Kings is a law to himself and in defiance of the Central Government will frequently undertake a raid on his own account. Sir Arnold Hodson quotes one such case in which the raiders captured no less than 8,000 slaves, the 'soldiers' being rewarded by being allowed to select one in every three slaves for themselves.

The raids between kingdom and kingdom of Abyssinia are doubtless on a much larger scale than those into the British territories of the Sudan, Kenya and Somaliland, but these are sometimes of a most serious character, more particularly when, as Captain Yardley points out, the result is the capture of British subjects and the murder of others. One of the latest of these raids was described to the House of Lords by Lord Hailsham, who pointed out that a serious double raid took place in March of last year, the raiders numbering 600 in all, that they attacked the Beir tribe and penetrated some fifty miles into the Upper Nile Province

[1] Sir Arnold Hodson, *Where Lion Reign.*

of the Sudan. As usual the men were put to death, the women and children carried off. Lord Hailsham said it was known that 27 men had been murdered, whilst 27 women and 50 children had been carried off.

Lord Noel-Buxton, whose interesting report upon the situation in Abyssinia has created a deep impression in the Chancellories of Europe, says that slave-raiding takes place chiefly in the Western Lowlands of Abyssinia, which are inhabited by negro or negroid tribes, and that these tribes are powerless to defend themselves in the face of well-armed raiding parties :

> These gentry shoot up the villages at night, when short shrift is given to older men and women, and the young natives of both sexes are carried off. Caravans are made up, and the captives are taken north, travelling by night, either to be disposed of in Abyssinia or to be embarked for Arabia. Slaves with black skins are preferred, because they are more easily tracked down if they escape. The Emperor's edicts have served to make the traffic less open ; business is driven from the market-place into the dark corners of the wattle huts. The illiterate natives are unable to read the edicts, which are posted in the villages. Moreover, administration in the Lowlands is practically non-existent. The hot and unhealthy climate of these regions is disliked by the Abyssinians, and they make haste to line their pockets by the sale of slaves which they have captured and which they dispose of on the road to Addis Ababa.

Only a few years ago a swashbuckling slaver boasted that he had ' left the road pretty '—' pretty ' with the blood and bones of murdered human beings. Slave routes are always left ' pretty ' by the slave-trader.

But for the slave the march along that road is always and at all times the march of torture and death. Is there anywhere in modern history anything more poignant than the picture of a slave gang travelling along a slave route as seen recently and portrayed for us by the German scientist, Herr Max Grühl ?

> We saw approaching a procession that defies the ablest pen to portray. Were they human ? One could hardly believe it. . . . Men and woman practically naked chained to one another, leading naked children by the hand or carrying them like bundles on their backs, dragged themselves through the filth and were driven like cattle by their heartless captors. Slaves ! A slave train in the twentieth century ! No figment of an overheated fancy, but human beings that had been torn from their homes, and dragged away to meet an unknown fate. Often falling by the wayside like sick animals. . . . If I had been able, I would have shot the slave-dealers as I would mad dogs. For hours the slave-train continued to pass us. Now, as I write these lines, our camp is surrounded by that of the robbers with hundreds of their captives. The rain is pouring down. But they have neither shelter nor fires nor food. Every now and then the clanking of chains echoes through the darkness.[1]

Will civilisation listen to the echo of those chains and send out to the sufferers in the darkness of the slave areas of the world a message of hope ?

There are those who would minimise the evils of slavery, those who discount the reports of travellers, but the testimony of men like Lord Noel-Buxton, Captain Yardley, Marcel Griaule, Herr Grühl, Sir Arnold Hodson cannot be lightly set on one side. This chapter depicting slavery as it is to-day could hardly find a more appropriate conclusion than in the following words written by Sir Arnold Hodson, the former Governor of Sierra Leone: 'These raids are even now occurring, and it will be understood how my blood boils when I read articles or letters in the Press, claiming that reports on slave-trade are grossly exaggerated.'

[1] Max Grühl, *The Citadel of Ethiopia*, 1932.

EPILOGUE

In the foregoing pages the reader has witnessed a cavalcade of men, women and children passing through one hundred years of misery, degradation, injustice, outrage and slaughter—in the main for sordid ends. The picture is indeed a dark one.

But it has another side—Abolitionists and Emancipators believed and believe that all men are equal in the sight of God, and that the doctrine 'there is no equality in Church or State between white and black' is a negation of the laws both of man and of God. In this belief they have fought on doggedly for a hundred years, winning battle after battle for right, and in doing so have established for Britain a truer title to fame than all her commercial and imperial greatness. In Lord Rosebery's words: 'I believe that this country when it stands before history, will stand, when all else has passed away, not by her fleets and her armies and her commerce, but by the heroic self-denying exertions which she has made to put down this iniquitous traffic.'

With humility, but with deep national thankfulness, let us take courage in the fact that within the last twenty years great things for native races have been accomplished under British leadership.

Under Britain's leadership the nations of the world have been persuaded to commit their respective countries to the doctrine that the treatment of native races is for civilisation—a Sacred Trust.

Under British leadership the nations of the world have been persuaded to sign a Treaty (the Slavery Convention), under which they have solemnly committed their countries to bring about the total suppression of slavery in all its forms throughout the world.

But it is one thing to sign treaties and to register pledges, it is quite another thing to get them carried out.

When the Maharajah of Nepal in his memorable speech of 1924 denounced slavery, he said ' the Curse of Heaven rests upon it.' It does indeed. When David Livingstone saw some of the things portrayed in this book he called down upon all who would help to remove that curse ' the Blessing of Heaven.' That all men might hearken to that message the British nation wrote it on his tomb in Westminster Abbey: ' May Heaven's rich blessing come down on every one —American, English or Turk—who will help to heal the open sore of the world.'

It is the fervent hope of the author that many a man and many a woman ' will help to heal the open sore ' of slavery and thereby enjoy the Blessing of Heaven.

APPENDIX

The Slavery Convention of the League of Nations, 1926

. . . . . .

Whereas the signatories of the General Act of the Brussels Conference of 1889–90 declared that they were equally animated by the firm intention of putting an end to the traffic in African slaves;

Whereas the signatories of the Convention of Saint Germain-en-Laye of 1919 to revise the General Act of Berlin of 1885 and the General Act and Declaration of Brussels of 1890 affirmed their intention of securing the complete suppression of slavery in all its forms and of the slave trade by land and sea;

Taking into consideration the report of the Temporary Slavery Commission appointed by the Council of the League of Nations on June 12th, 1924;

Desiring to complete and extend the work accomplished under the Brussels Act and to find a means of giving practical effect throughout the world to such intentions as were expressed in regard to slave trade and slavery by the signatories of the Convention of Saint Germain-en-Laye, and recognising that it is necessary to conclude to that end more detailed arrangements than are contained in that Convention;

Considering, moreover, that it is necessary to prevent forced labour from developing into conditions analogous to slavery;

Have decided to conclude a Convention and have accordingly appointed as their Plenipotentiaries :

. . . . . .

Who, having communicated their full powers, have agreed as follows :

Article 1.

For the purpose of the present Convention, the following definitions are agreed upon :

1. Slavery is the status or condition of a person over whom any or all of the powers attaching to the right of ownership are exercised.

2. The slave trade includes all acts involved in the capture, acquisition or disposal of a person with intent to reduce him to slavery ; all acts involved in the acquisition of a slave with a view to selling or exchanging him ; all acts of disposal by sale or exchange of a slave acquired with a view to being sold or exchanged, and, in general, every act of trade or transport in slaves.

Article 2.

The High Contracting Parties undertake, each in respect of the territories placed under its sovereignty, jurisdiction, protection, suzerainty or tutelage, so far as they have not already taken the necessary steps :

(*a*) To prevent and suppress the slave trade ;

(*b*) To bring about, progressively and as soon as possible, the complete abolition of slavery in all its forms.

Article 3.

The High Contracting Parties undertake to adopt all appropriate measures with a view to preventing and suppressing the embarkation, disembarkation and transport of slaves in their territorial waters and upon all vessels flying their respective flags.

The High Contracting Parties undertake to negotiate

as soon as possible a general Convention with regard to the slave trade which will give them rights and impose upon them duties of the same nature as those provided for in the Convention of June 17th, 1925, relative to the International Trade in Arms (Articles 12, 20, 21, 22, 23, 24, and paragraphs 3, 4 and 5 of Section II of Annex II) with the necessary adaptations, it being understood that this general Convention will not place the ships (even of small tonnage) of any High Contracting Parties in a position different from that of the other High Contracting Parties.

It is also understood that, before or after the coming into force of this general Convention, the High Contracting Parties are entirely free to conclude between themselves, without, however, derogating from the principles laid down in the preceding article, such special agreements as, by reason of their peculiar situation, might appear to be suitable in order to bring about as soon as possible the complete disappearance of the slave trade.

Article 4.

The High Contracting Parties shall give to one another every assistance with the object of securing the abolition of slavery and the slave trade.

Article 5.

The High Contracting Parties recognise that recourse to compulsory or forced labour may have grave consequences and undertake, each in respect of the territories placed under its sovereignty, jurisdiction, protection, suzerainty or tutelage, to take all necessary measures to prevent compulsory or forced labour from developing into conditions analogous to slavery.

It is agreed that:

(1) Subject to the transitional provisions laid down in paragraph (2) below, compulsory or forced labour may only be exacted for public purposes.

(2) In territories in which compulsory or forced labour for other than public purposes still survives, the High Contracting Parties shall endeavour progressively and as soon as possible to put an end to the practice. So long as such forced or compulsory labour exists, this labour shall invariably be of an exceptional character, shall always receive adequate remuneration, and shall not involve the removal of the labourers from their usual place of residence.

(3) In all cases, the responsibility for any recourse to compulsory or forced labour shall rest with the competent central authorities of the territory concerned.

Article 6.

Those of the High Contracting Parties whose laws do not at present make adequate provision for the punishment of infractions of laws and regulations enacted with a view to giving effect to the purposes of the present Convention undertake to adopt the necessary measures in order that severe penalties may be imposed in respect of such infractions.

Article 7.

The High Contracting Parties undertake to communicate to each other and to the Secretary-General of the League of Nations any laws and regulations which they may enact with a view to the application of the provisions of the present Convention.

Article 8.

The High Contracting Parties agree that disputes arising between them relating to the interpretation or application of this Convention shall, if they cannot be settled by direct negotiation, be referred for decision to the Permanent Court of International Justice. In case either or both of the States Parties to such a dispute should not be parties to the Protocol of December 16th, 1920, relating to the Permanent Court of International Justice, the dispute shall be referred, at the choice of the Parties and in accordance with the constitutional procedure of each State, either to the Permanent Court of International Justice or to a court of arbitration constituted in accordance with the Convention of October 18th, 1907, for the Pacific Settlement of International Disputes, or to some other court of arbitration.

Article 9.

At the time of signature or of ratification or of accession, any High Contracting Party may declare that its acceptance of the present Convention does not bind some or all of the territories placed under its sovereignty, jurisdiction, protection, suzerainty or tutelage in respect of all or any provisions of the Convention ; it may subsequently accede separately on behalf of any one of them or in respect of any provision to which any one of them is not a party.

Article 10.

In the event of a High Contracting Party wishing to denounce the present Convention, the denunciation shall be notified in writing to the Secretary-General of the League of Nations, who will at once communicate a certified true copy of the notification to all the other High Contracting Parties informing them of the date on which it was received.

The denunciation shall only have effect in regard to the notifying State, and one year after the notification has reached the Secretary-General of the League of Nations.

Denunciation may also be made separately in respect of any territory placed under its sovereignty, jurisdiction, protection, suzerainty or tutelage.

Article 11.

The present Convention, which will bear this day's date and of which the French and English texts are both authentic, will remain open for signature by the States Members of the League of Nations until April 1st, 1927.

The Secretary-General of the League of Nations will subsequently bring the present Convention to the notice of States which have not signed it, including States which are not Members of the League of Nations, and invite them to accede thereto.

A State desiring to accede to the Convention shall notify its intention in writing to the Secretary-General of the League of Nations and transmit to him the instrument of accession, which shall be deposited in the archives of the League.

The Secretary-General shall immediately transmit to all the other High Contracting Parties a certified true copy of the notification and of the instrument of accession, informing them of the date on which he received them.

Article 12.

The present Convention will be ratified and the instruments of ratification shall be deposited in the office of the Secretary-General of the League of Nations. The Secretary-General will inform all the High Contracting Parties of such deposit.

The Convention will come into operation for each State on the date of the deposit of its ratification or of its accession.

In faith whereof the Plenipotentiaries have signed the present Convention.

DONE at Geneva the twenty-fifth day of September, one thousand nine hundred and twenty-six, in one copy, which will be deposited in the archives of the League of Nations. A certified copy shall be forwarded to each signatory State.

INDEX

I 3